Thinking about Political Things

An Aristotelian Approach to Pacific Life

Andrew Murray SM

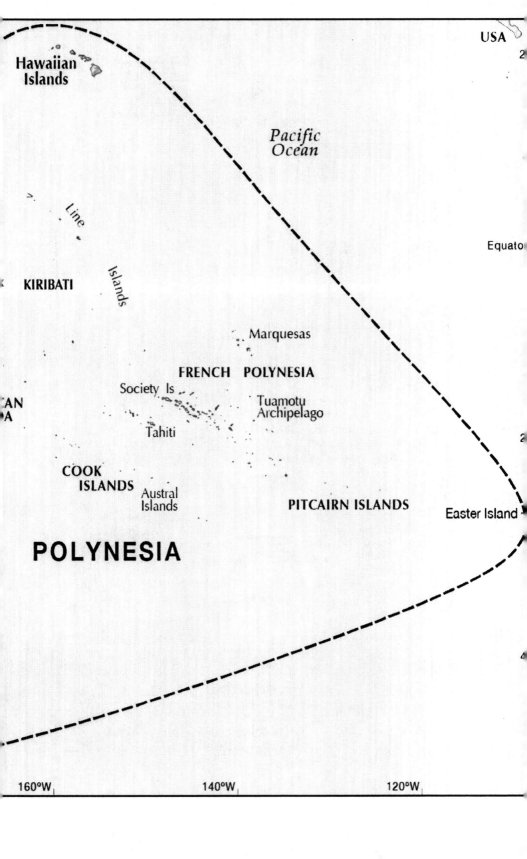

Text copyright © 2016 remains with the author.

Title: Thinking about political things : an Aristotelian approach to
Pacific life / Andrew Peter Murray.

ISBN: 9781925232981 (paperback)
ISBN 9781925232998 hardback
ISBN 9781925232001 epub
ISBN 9781925232025 pdf
ISBN 9781925232018 kindle

Series: Marist series ; vol. 6.
Notes: Includes index.
Subjects: Aristotle.--Ethics.
Aristotle--Contributions in political science.
Political ethics.
Islands of the Pacific--Politics and government--Philosophy.

Dewey Number: 320.01

The Marist Series

Through the Marist Series the Society of Mary (Marist Fathers) shares projects by
Marists in the field of theology and history and works about the role of the Marists
in the church, in particular in the Pacific.

Series Editor: Alois Greiler SM

1. *Catholic Beginnings in Oceania: Marist Missionary Perspectives*, 2009, edited by
   Alois Greiler SM.
2. *A Mission Too Far . . . Pacific Commitment and the Missions 1835–1841*, 2012,
   Jan Snijders SM.
3. *Thinking Things Through: Essays in Philosophy and Christian Faith*, 2102,
   Andrew Murray SM.
4. *Verguet's Sketchbook*, 2014, Mervyn Duffy SM and Alois Greiler SM.
5. *Letters from the Marist Missionaries in Oceania 1836-1854*, 2016, Charles
   Girard SM.

Cover: Photo by the author on the island of Pororan, Bougainville.

An imprint of ATF Ltd.
PO Box 504
Hindmarsh, SA 5007
ABN 90 116 359 963
www.atfpress.com

Thinking about Political Things

An Aristotelian Approach to Pacific Life

Andrew Murray SM

ATF Theology
Adelaide
2016

To Chief John Momis

and

In memory of Michael Kouro of Siwai

Contents

Preface

My purpose in writing this book was to express Aristotle's political thought in clear non-technical language and in ways that would assist the peoples of small island states, particularly in the Pacific, to think about the political issues that face them. As I explain in the introductory chapter, their political problems and the solutions that they have either found or will need to find are different from those of large Western countries. This book nevertheless remains a work in philosophy, and as I always tell students beginning their study in philosophy, one has to read a philosophy book several times in order to make full sense of it. It is about thinking, and thinking is a contemplative exercise.

Four essays, each of which I will call an *excursion*, stand outside the flow of the philosophical narrative and are placed between chapters. Each excursion is a journey to a particular place and examines the life of the people there in the light of a particular political concern. The excursions can, therefore, be read alone or read as illustrating in more detail how the theory expounded in the chapters might be applied to more practical situations. They show how someone educated in classical political philosophy would think about the issues. The excursions are informed by actual visits to the places discussed, and each uses different academic resources and methods. The first excursion uses popular and academic literature to explore the *wantok* system of Papua New Guinea and the Solomon Islands. The second excursion looks at the constitutional history of Fiji by examining the four constitutions it has had since 1970. The third excursion takes just two histories of Tonga and examines how chance and change have made it what it is today. It shows the importance of history for understanding political things and how one can make good use of even limited resources. The fourth excursion investigates the cultural identity of the Chamorro people of the Mariana Islands, using various literatures and informed with a sympathy engendered by an extended visit to the islands.

Several people have read and commented on earlier drafts of either the entire manuscript or parts of it: Soane 'Ahohako, David Arms, Matthew Del Nevo, Phillip Gibbs, William Grey, Bal Kama, Peter Lamour, Lawrence McCane, Clive Moore, Kevin Murray, Michael O'Connor, John Owens, Mikaele Paunga, Anthony Percy, Epeli Qimaqima, Rapin Quinn, Mary Roddy, John Rohan, and Robert Sokolowski. I am grateful that their examinations were thorough and that their suggestions have resulted in a much improved text. I am also grateful to my students at Catholic Institute of Sydney, who have wrestled with the issues in the Social and Political Philosophy course over many years and to my students in the Politics in Melanesia course at Catholic Theological Institute at Bomana, Papua New Guinea, and at Holy Name Seminary in Honiara, Solomon Islands.

This book began with *ex gratia* study leave in 2003, which enabled a close study of Aristotle's *Politics* and resulted in an earlier book, *What Can the Church Say? Religion and Politics in Contemporary Australia*. In 2005, a funded sabbatical enabled me to make extended visits to several Pacific countries and to test my ideas. Further *ex gratia* study leave in 2009 enabled the philosophical chapters to be substantially written. I am grateful to Catholic Institute of Sydney for making these opportunities available. I am also grateful to the Marist Fathers for their encouragement and for the opportunity to spend time in the Pacific.

The State, Society and Governance Program (SSGM) at the Australian National University was most generous in granting me a Visiting Fellowship from 2012–14. This allowed me access to library resources without which the four excursions could not have been written. Richard Eves was my mentor, and Anthony Regan was always generous with his time and thought. David Hegarty and Bill Standish have been most hospitable during the decade of my interaction with SSGM. I have also profited from SSGM seminars, workshops and conferences over a longer period of time. The fellowship gave me access to the CartoGIS unit in the College of Asia and the Pacific at ANU, and I am grateful to them for the use of their maps and especially to Jennifer Sheehan, who produced the particular set that I include in this book.

Chapter One
Introduction

In contemporary political and academic discourse, one often hears the terms 'weak state' or 'failed state'. Leaders of Pacific countries are discomforted but also legitimately annoyed when these terms are applied to their own countries. On the one hand, most of these countries are not and probably cannot become the great economic machines that are so much part of the modern world and that sustain larger and more powerful states. There is often dissatisfaction in such countries with how services and resources are delivered and confusion about what centralised government should achieve for national life. On the other hand, leaders in the Pacific can point out that in their countries people do not for the most part go hungry or remain unhoused as they might do in Sydney or London or New York. People are connected to their clans and on fertile islands they can easily grow food. Their annoyance is however justified, because the 'weak state' criticism masks the assumption that small states, and Pacific states in particular, should become instances of the Modern European State.

The political form known as the *Modern European State* is a product of a particular history and of human intervention that came together in Europe during the seventeenth century. Events that were significant in its formation include: the Treaty of Westphalia in 1648, which ended the post-Reformation religious wars and set down firm state borders; various revolutions, especially the French Revolution of 1789–99, and their calls for a new radical form of democracy; the collapse of the old monarchies and feudal land systems; the industrial revolution of the eighteenth and nineteenth centuries; and the emergence of people who thought of themselves as 'individuals' rather than as members of families and clans or as adherents to a religious community. These events and the practical resolutions by politicians of the problems they raised were accompanied by intense theoretical speculation by people such as Machiavelli, Bodin, Hobbes, Locke, Rousseau, Kant and Hegel.

The Modern European State has become the dominant political form in the contemporary world, even though there are significant variations in the way in which the form has been applied in different countries. It has been attractive for its ability to cope with very large populations and for the impetus it gives to economic activity, both in providing incentive to those who would engage in industry and in offering protection to enterprises that are dependent on large amounts of capital. It has enabled new senses of freedom in which citizens have been able to claim the right to live as they prefer. It has brought a kind of peace within states based on strong government, control of the instruments of force and freedom to express ideas. Contrarily, as we have seen in the twentieth century, it has allowed or even fostered dreadful wars between states and enabled the rise of vicious totalitarian regimes.

The Modern European State has nevertheless been based on dubious assumptions such as claims that people can be understood only as individuals and not as members of families and clans; that life will be good if the means are provided whereby all individuals are able to satisfy whatever desires move them; that these desires are generally of a material nature; that perpetual economic growth is necessary; that radical democracy is the best form of government; that politics can be free of ethical concerns. It is these sorts of beliefs that often sit uncomfortably with peoples in traditional cultures, and the work of this book will in part be to investigate an alternative way of thinking about political life.

This book will attempt to articulate the political thought of Aristotle as found in his work, the *Politics*, as well as in his other works, especially the *Nicomachean Ethics* and the *Rhetoric*. The book's thesis is that an Aristotelian way of thinking will provide a more adequate way for Pacific Islanders to examine first the best way to live and secondly how to achieve appropriate forms of government given their current circumstances. The political problem of determining how a people in a particular place at a particular time can best live and create laws that will allow all members of a large community to participate in common life, and to flourish as human beings, has not been solved once and for all by the Modern European State or by any other political form. Rather, it is a problem that needs to be solved by practical wisdom and by judgements made by political leaders, legislators and citizens in each place and time.[1]

Aristotle did not lay down a particular political form as necessary for all peoples in the way that early modern theorists did. Rather, he recognised that political communities grow out of natural communities and that they are formed with particular senses of the good and of what constitutes a good life. What they can achieve is moderated by conditions and circumstances such as geography, history, culture, economic possibility and the availability of people able to judge and act wisely. His thought surveys a range of formal possibilities—monarchy, aristocracy, republicanism, democracy, oligarchy and tyranny—and shows how these forms might be blended in particular instances. It is, therefore, not a formula but rather instruction in how to think about issues. My thesis is that Pacific peoples may find political forms more suited to their situation and preferred kinds of life through this kind of analysis rather than through unreflective adoption of some form of the Modern European State.[2]

Aristotle was a Greek who lived from 384 to 322 BC. He was born at Stagira in Macedonia but spent much of his life studying and

1. I am deeply indebted in this project to Robert Sokolowski and particularly to his article, 'The Human Person and Political Life', in Robert Sokolowski, *Christian Faith and Human Understanding: Studies on the Eucharist, Trinity and the Human Person* (Washington, DC: Catholic University of America Press, 2006), chapter 12, pages 179–98. The article was also published in *The Thomist: A Speculative Quarterly Review* 65/4 (October 2001): 505–27.
2. This project was first proposed at the Pacific Interreligious Colloquium on Indigenous Cultural and Religious Concepts of Peace and Good Governance, Tofamamao Centre, Samoa, 28–30 December 2005. See Tui Atua Tupua Tamasese Taisi Efi, Tamasailau M Suaalii et al., editors, 'Room to Move: Thoughts from Political Philosophy', in *Pacific Indigenous Dialogue on Faith, Reconciliation and Good Governance*, Alafua Campus Continuing and Community Education Programme (Apia, Samoa: University of the South Pacific Press, 2007), chapter 21, pages 196–9. Early investigation of the project had been undertaken at a seminar in the Business Faculty of the University of Papua New Guinea. I am grateful to the people involved in these events for their ideas and encouragement then and since.

teaching in Athens. He was taught by the great philosopher, Plato, and inspired by Socrates, whom many recognise as the founder of the Western philosophical tradition. Philosophy began as the science that attempts to understand all things in their broadest context and therefore the relationships between different kinds of things. Philosophy deals not only with what is actual but also with what is possible, so that a vital philosophical imagination is a wonderful tool for examining the world and human life and asking how things are, how might they be and how they best would be.

It is fair to ask why we might turn to an author who wrote so long ago and in a different place. There are three lines of argument for this. First, as I have already suggested, Aristotle's politics is non-coercive. He does not tell citizens and politicians what to do but rather helps them to think about the matters concerning which they need to make sound practical judgements. Secondly, Aristotle wrote his *Politics* at a time when the experience of political life that allowed for the participation of citizens, the Greek democracy, was fresh in the Greek world and with the assistance of his forebears he was able to analyse what was happening. There were many Greek states spread out across the Aegean Sea, and although some were stronger than others, they were all small and each had a slightly different experience. It was a particular historical moment when political realities were revealed most clearly not just in terms of what was happening then but also in terms of the possibilities of politics as such. Thirdly, Aristotle had a gift that is rare in human history for seeing the truth of things and being able to articulate it in language that reveals it to others. Someone like Shakespeare also had this gift, and when we read his plays, we are often able to cut through the confusion and obscurity of our own vision of things so as to grasp the fine lines of human thought, action and feeling. Aristotle does this in his philosophical writings, which show a singular capacity to make the right distinctions, to exhibit common sense, to view all sides of a question and to be moderate in judgement.

Objection may also be raised to the fact that most of this book is expressed in terms of what Aristotle taught. Why not draw on other significant philosophers? In fact, the book does draw on other philosophers. As we will see in Chapter Three, Aristotle himself examined, criticised and learnt from the views of his contemporaries.

The book itself draws on a number of modern philosophers generally by way of criticism and contrast. Yet it remains true that the main line of argument in the book is presented in Aristotle's voice. There is a philosophical reason for this. Philosophy attempts to articulate a coherent account of the whole of the reality that it deals with. It is especially concerned with the consistency of the main lines of its argument. This is best achieved by one mind, and we are lucky that Aristotle was able to do it. Philosophical method, therefore, contrasts with the more technical sciences, in which ideas, distinctions or mechanisms can be borrowed from multiple sources and put together piece by piece. This can be useful and indeed necessary, but the philosophical stance enables us to be clearer on where we are heading before we begin to build the parts.

For Aristotle, political science or the study of politics is intimately related to ethics. In fact, the last chapter of his major ethical work, the *Nicomachean Ethics*, which we will simply call the *Ethics*, serves as a transition and introduction to the *Politics*, which necessarily follows from it. Each of the books begins by raising the question of good. 'Every art and every investigation and similarly every action and pursuit, is considered to aim at some good.'[3] So begins the *Ethics*, which goes on to investigate human happiness, the virtues, friendship and pleasure. The *Politics* begins similarly. 'Since we see that every [country] is some sort of [community], and that every [community] is constituted for the sake of some good . . . it is clear that all [communities] aim at some good.'[4] The concern of each is the same—the *good* that is the object of action. In the *Ethics*, it is personal action that is at stake; in the *Politics*, it is the action of and indeed the very formation of the community.

There is an essential link between the two. Aristotle points out at the end of the *Ethics* that it is not enough to know about goodness: one must possess it and become good. He canvasses views about how one becomes good—by nature, by instruction and by habit. Nature he leaves, because although some may have a natural aptitude for good

3. Aristotle, *The Nicomachean Ethics* I, 1 (1094a1), translated by JAK Thomson and revised by Hugh Tredennick (London: Penguin, 2004), 3.
4. Aristotle, *The Politics* I, 1 (1252a1), translated with an introduction by Carnes Lord (Chicago: University of Chicago Press, 1984), 35, substituting 'country' for 'city' and 'community' for 'partnership'. See comment on translation at the end of Chapter One.

action, it is a gift not given to most, and because just having a natural aptitude does not make us good. We need to activate it and to make it our own. Instruction may teach people what is good, but generally their feelings and desires will pull them in other ways. And so, habituation, whereby people are moved to act in the best ways until these ways of acting become second nature to them, is critical. Ideally, this happens in the family, but it should also happen at the level of the political community, so that consistent ways of acting are instilled in people through laws and customs as well as by punishment.

To form a coherent community with good laws is the work of a politician or statesman. It is a practical achievement calling for the ability to assist many people not related by blood to act together to form good institutions and good laws. The problems are many, and so the experience of the statesman is important. The political scientist, on the other hand, can assist by clarifying what is at stake and by examining successful and failed attempts to be successful. This is what Aristotle sets out to do in the *Politics*. His hope is that with some assistance politicians and citizens will be able to develop communities in which all citizens can flourish intellectually, socially, economically and morally.

Although this seems fairly straightforward, it is not necessarily a common view, at least in the modern West. It was Niccolò Machiavelli (1469–1527) who pushed understandings in a different direction. In *The Prince*, he proposed that we no longer imagine that we can organise communities that might facilitate the formation of virtue. 'The fact is that a man who wants to act virtuously in every way necessarily comes to grief among so many who are not virtuous.'[5] Machiavelli's influence has flowed in muted form into the presuppositions of modern liberal democracy, in which matters of ethics and custom are seen as outside the scope of government unless some harm or conflict affecting other citizens is involved. In following Aristotelian presuppositions, we will keep open a wider perspective.

The aim of this book is to make Aristotle's political teaching available for politicians and citizens who have an interest in finding ways to think about the problems that face them in working to make their countries function effectively and well, so that their people can

---

5. Niccolò Machiavelli, *The Prince*, translated by George Bull (London: Penguin, 2003), chapter 15, page 50.

flourish. It is, therefore, a work of political education. Its imagined first audience is the people of Pacific countries, who live mostly on small islands in a vast sea and whose traditional cultures are often at odds with modern Western culture. Other audiences will be people in similar situations in other parts of the world. Indeed, even those intent on being thoughtful about problems experienced in the West will find this work helpful. More particularly, however, the aim of the book is to make Aristotle's thought available in readable form for people not specifically trained in philosophy.

The book is, therefore, not an attempt to tell Pacific peoples what to do in their political lives. Decisions about various political arrangements and about how to manage relationships within a political community belong to the people themselves and to their leaders. If they are 'blessed', they will have prudent and able leaders to guide them. An outsider can see certain things but can never fully understand the sensibilities of a culture nor the deeper interests of different people and groups in the community. Rather, the book offers a way of thinking about political issues in the hope that it will enable Pacific peoples to resolve their own difficulties and to chart their own courses. It is therefore a work of political philosophy and will spend much of its time articulating the thought of Aristotle.

Nevertheless, examples from countries of the South Pacific will be used in a way that will show the relevance of the Aristotelian manner of thinking about political things and that will suggest how it might inform the thinking of people and politicians. This will be done in two ways. First, examples will be used within the chapters to illustrate the points that are being made. Secondly, the four excursions will be inserted between chapters to examine specific Pacific issues or problems in greater detail. These can be regarded as separate from the flow of argument in the chapters and so can be read in whatever order suits the reader.

The text of Aristotle's *Politics* is not easy to master. It is dense. Often discussions seem incomplete. It seems to begin a number of times, at least in Books I, II, III, IV and VII. Scholars have wrestled with this. Some have rearranged the text assuming that there had been confusion in the manuscript tradition. Others have suggested that parts have been lost. An alternative view is suggested by Aristotle himself when he articulates the principle that a small error at the

beginning will have great effect at the end, emphasising that the work
of the philosopher is to clarify beginnings and to make the formal
lines of an argument clear.[6] To deal with all the details would be too
much and somewhat pointless, because 'speaking about them is a
work of prayer; having them come about, a work of chance'.[7] As well,
Aristotle insists that in the area of political science only a limited
degree of precision is possible.[8] It is, rather, the task of the legislator
and politician to master the particularities of a given situation and
to put in place law and policy that achieve what is possible in the
circumstances. Aristotle refers many times to the *Politics* as 'these
discourses', and that is what they are—discussions of critical issues
that will give politicians and citizens direction as they undertake their
deliberations about law and constitution.

Because the main project of this book is to present the political
thought of Aristotle in outline fashion in a manner accessible to non-
philosophers, the chapters will follow the *Politics* closely, though with
significant change in their sequence, in order to provide an orderly
first account of Aristotle's thought. Scholarly apparatus will be kept to
a minimum, though commentaries and other literature will be listed
in the bibliography. It is hoped that some of those who read the book
will, in time, go on to study Aristotle's work itself. A reader who finds
interest in a particular discussion may wish to go immediately to
Aristotle's own text. For that reason, a table is provided in Appendix
One to link the chapters and sections of the book to the specific texts of
Aristotle on which they rely. An outline of the *Politics* is also provided
in Appendix Two. Moreover, as further aids to readers, comparative
geographic, demographic, economic and political data for the various
Pacific island nations are provided in Appendix Three, and Appendix
Four supplies maps of the region at various scales.

---

6.   Aristotle, *Politics* V, 4 (1303b28), 153. See also Aristotle, *On the Heavens* I, 5
     (271b8–13), in *The Complete Works of Aristotle: The Revised Oxford Translation*,
     edited by Jonathan Barnes (Princeton, NJ: Princeton University Press, 1985),
     where the point is made more strongly. Thomas Aquinas draws on Aristotle
     to make this point at the beginning of his *On Being and Essence*. See *On Being
     and Essence*, translated by Armand Maurer (Toronto: Pontifical Institute of
     Mediaeval Studies, 1983), prologue, 28.
7.   Aristotle, *Politics* VII, 12 (1331b18–20), 216.
8.   Aristotle, *Ethics* I, 2–3.

Finally, by way of introduction, there is some difficulty in translating some of Aristotle's terms into modern English, and often translations carry with them theoretical positions. At times, this will be noted in the text but a few terms can be noted here. *Koinonia*, I have translated as 'community' rather than as 'association' or 'partnership'. *Polis*, which is often translated 'city' or 'city-state' and which was the political entity most known to Aristotle, I have translated as 'country', which today best grasps the Aristotelian sense of the whole political entity. Aristotle uses *politeia* in two ways. For the first, I will use 'constitution' rather than 'regime'; for the second I will use 'republic' rather than 'polity', which is a less familiar English word. In giving quotations from the *Politics*, I will use the translation of Carnes Lord in each instance, but with the above changes where they apply.[9]

---

9. Substitutions of these terms will be noted in the footnotes.

Chapter Two
Kinds of Lives and the Origins of Political Community

How are we to understand politics or political life? It is with this kind of question that Aristotle begins his *Politics*, and he quickly establishes important parameters and lines of investigation. He will examine the political community itself. Then he will look at its parts, in the first instance the parts that are original in the sense that they precede the formation of a political community. He will ask about its end—why does it exist, or what does it seek to achieve? He will examine the material needs of this community. He will examine the different kinds of rule or leadership that are part of human life and of political life in particular. Informing this discussion will be an understanding of human nature and of human beings.

It is important that Aristotle begins with the political community, because it is a concrete entity, the political order that actually exists rather than something simply imagined. In Aristotle's situation, it was the *polis* or city, which developed in Greece around small communities living in places such as Athens and Sparta. Here the city and surrounding countryside were formed into a community that was largely self-sufficient and strong enough to establish firm relations with its neighbours. That these cities governed themselves in ways that enabled broad participation was a relatively new accomplishment and something that was clearly exciting to Aristotle. In today's world, we call the equivalent political community living in a certain territory, whose members participate in various ways in its governance, a *country*.

Aristotle's study gets its realism from studying actually existing communities, but it does not stop there. Real communities sometimes do well and sometimes do badly. Aristotle's study is not simply empirical but rather philosophical and will gradually unfold the most appropriate distinctions and discover the underlying principles. By uncovering these formal structures of things, Aristotle will give us clear lines for thinking without overwhelming us with masses of detail. From this investigation he will be able to assist us to think about what possibilities are best and how we might achieve them.

Pre-Political Communities

In his first look at the parts of a political community, Aristotle distinguishes the household and the village. We might call these *pre-political communities*, and they carry with them their own kinds of life—family life and village or clan life. In contrast to ideas about the modern state, which see individuals as the only constituent elements of the state, Aristotle recognises these pre-political communities as natural and as essential parts of the political community. We could list other kinds of pre-political communities, such as churches, clubs and what we call today non-government organisations (NGOs).[1] Not all of these would be natural, but from the Aristotelian point of view they are communities that are parts of a country and are necessary for its good functioning. They need to be taken into account in any set of political arrangements. For now, however, we will look at the primitive and more essential communities.

The *household*, or we might say the *family*, is the first community, and it is natural and necessary. It is natural in the sense that it comes into being through the natural desire between a man and a woman that leads to the birth of children. It is necessary because it supplies daily human needs and because the development of children is slow and requires constant care. The essential relationships are between husband and wife, and parents and children. Aristotle does not imagine that parents and children could survive just on their own, and so his household also includes servants.[2] In the context of his

---

1. NGOs can be either grassroots (or recipient) NGOs or international (or donor) NGOs. They can be further defined in so far as they interact with the needs of the people in affiliation with the state, business, or local communities. See Rapin Quinn, 'NGOs, Peasants and the State: Transformation and Intervention in Rural Thailand, 1970–1990' (unpublished PhD dissertation, Australian National University, Canberra, 1997).
2. The word that Aristotle uses is usually translated as 'slave', but there is not in

time, one can imagine a country estate owned by the family but including servants, who labour in the fields and assist around the house. Nowadays we tend not to have servants, although we may employ people to help with house work, and in some Pacific countries, members of the extended family will live in the same household and give practical support. Western cities have developed far more isolated living, in which only the immediate family lives in a house, but these households are dependent on very complex forms of employment, services and commerce that only modern cities and towns can provide. They also depend on motor vehicles for the rapid transport of people and materials.

A *village* is formed when several households get together to form a single community. Aristotle's view is that this is for the sake of supplying and helping with non-daily needs. In other words, the household retains responsibility for daily food and care, but in the village there is the possibility of assistance with other things, such as house building and transport, and also of other human advantages such as the opportunity to have conversation, to play sport or to join in communal activities. Aristotle's view is that these first villages grow out of family or clan groups, so that most families would be somehow related to one another. The kind of rule or leadership he envisages is monarchical—the rule of a king or chief—because the people are bound by affection and because the respect that exists in these small communities readily recognises the one who is senior.

Political Community

A *political community* arises when a number of villages or groups of villages come together to form one community, which is of a very different kind from a household or a single village. Aristotle tells us that the political community is formed not just for the sake of living

---

Greek a separate word for 'servant'. Slavery of different kinds was an institution in the ancient world. I will argue in the next section and have argued elsewhere that 'servant' is a better translation of the form of life that Aristotle would seem to support, just as he argues against most other forms of slavery. See Andrew Murray, 'Freedom, Nature and Slavery in Aristotle's *Politics*', in *God, Freedom and Nature: Proceedings of the Biennial Conference in Philosophy, Religion and Culture*, edited by RS Laura, RA Buchanan and A Chapman (Boston: Body and Soul Dynamics, 2012), 83–8.

but for the sake of living well. It enables a level of self-sufficiency not possible in single villages, but more importantly it responds to the rationality of the human being, which is revealed by speech. Human beings are not just animals, which have needs of food and shelter, but they have minds that are turned towards investigating the truth about what is good and what is just. Speech enables them to carry on this investigation in collaboration with others, who in the political community are not simply family members. This is what Aristotle means when he says that human beings are 'political animals'.[3] And so the end of a political community is to allow for the full flowering of human nature. The question of what flourishing means is the question of the good—what are the intellectual, moral and material goods that human beings seek? It is a question that we will take up in more detail in Chapters Five and Ten.

When I was in Bougainville in 2005, a secondary-school student asked me, why should we bother with government? Why not just live in a house or village in the bush? It was a good question, because during the time of the Bougainville Crisis (1989–98), when Bougainville was blockaded by the Papua New Guinea Defence Force, families had learnt to live alone or in small villages in the bush. With good food and relative isolation from infectious diseases, they even found that their general health had improved. Aristotle's answer is that by living in the larger political community we have the opportunity to live richer lives in which our full human potential is allowed to flourish. This may be through learning and schooling or through the kind of interaction with others that enables us to solve problems and to find ways of living and working together well. It is not only that this kind of community brings us more and better material goods and services but also that it facilitates a better kind of life.

It is for this reason that Aristotle says that the political community is natural. It arises because it alone enables the realisation of full human capability. He says, 'One who is incapable of participating or who is in need of nothing through being self-sufficient is no part of a [country], and so is either a beast or a god'.[4] He even goes so far as to say that the political community is prior to the household. This is not a priority of time or origin but rather a priority of end. It is only in a

3.   See Aristotle, *Politics* I, 2 (1253a2), 37; III, 6 (1278b19), 94.
4.   Aristotle, *Politics* I, 2 (1253a28), 37, substituting 'country' for 'city'.

well-functioning political community that human beings can achieve their full potential—truth, friendship and justice—and so they are by nature drawn to this kind of community. The common good consists in human beings acting together in excellent ways. Unlike the household, however, the political community does not come to be by itself. It has to be formed and organised by human activity, which can be done well or badly. For this reason, Aristotle bestows high praise on founders of cities who have put together successful regimes. The purpose of the study of politics is, therefore, to teach people how to think about the issues involved in such an enterprise so that they will make good practical judgements in constructing or adjusting the arrangements of their communities.

Different Kinds of Rule

One of the things that people find shocking when they first read Aristotle's *Politics* is his treatment of slavery, which was a prevalent institution in his time. While Aristotle rejected many forms of slavery and probably the notion that there could be family lines that would always be slaves, he argues that some people are naturally suited to be what we call *servants*. Indeed, he finds a place for them in the household. At first sight this is strange, because the end of the political community is to enable people to be free and to exercise judgement about their future, and so we need to understand his reasons. Aristotle gives three reasons why some people will be servants. First, some people lack foresight and the ability to plan ahead, so that they are better working under a master, who is able to plan ahead. Secondly, some people lack the spirit or energy to be free, while others are eager to govern. Thirdly, the material things we need, such as food and shelter, are perishable, so that part of the human condition is to be engaged in continual labour. The two truths that we find here are that there are differences in human capacity and that the satisfaction of human needs demands constant labour. These together constitute an impetus towards subjection, in which some are 'employed' by others. Even though Christian thought about the dignity of the human person and the modern political concern with universal human rights argue against this view, Aristotle has exposed a critical point that has to be taken into account when we think about the nature and arrangement of the political community.

We have now looked at three kinds of community—the household, the village and the political community or country. We could also say that these engender three kinds of life—family life, village life and national life—in each of which we share. They are different and call for different patterns of action and different skills. We have noted different relationships that are found in these communities. These different relationships generate different kinds of rule or ways of exercising leadership, and it is these that we must examine now. Again, staying with essential lines of difference rather than the many actual instances, Aristotle suggests five general kinds of rule.

The first is *matrimonial rule*, which is found between husband and wife. Aristotle believes that the man usually rules but sees the relationship as participatory or political so that there is discussion and agreement, and he allows for areas of household life that are the proper domain of the woman. The second is the *rule of parents over children*, which is marked by the fact that children are not fully developed human beings, so that it is a relation of care, sometimes monarchical but allowing for the development of freedom. The third is *mastery* or the rule of master over servant, in which the master plans for the future and the servant follows instructions about what is to be done now and generally contributes labour. The fourth is *monarchical rule* or the rule of king or chief over subjects. The fifth is *political rule*, which is the rule of citizens, who are free and who expect to participate in decisions about the life of the community. These are profoundly different ways of ruling or exercising leadership, and it is important that we act correctly according to the kind of relationship in which we are engaged. Part of the complexity of human life is that we may find that we engage with all five different kinds of rule in different parts of our lives or even simultaneously. We therefore need to be able to adjust our ways of thinking and acting. Aristotle says that there are virtues proper to each kind of rule. We will deal with just the last three kinds of rule in this chapter and with the first two in Chapters Eight and Nine.

Taking these three in reverse order, *political rule* is the rule of citizens, who lay claim to sharing in the action of the community. They expect to participate in decisions about future activities and to be able to form judgements about past events. They live lives actively engaged with the affairs of the community. Not all can rule at once, and Aristotle often reiterates that the art of being a citizen is to know how 'to rule and to be ruled'. Citizens share functions in such a way that at one time one will be ruling the other and that at another time the roles will be reversed. They therefore need considerable skills in order to be able to live in this way. *Monarchical* or *chiefly rule* is the rule of subjects who are not citizens. It is exercised by one who carries the respect of the community and is for the sake of the community as a whole and of each of the people in it. The monarch stands for the community in a more vivid way than could, for instance, an elected assembly. Aristotle recognises monarchical rule as beneficial both for small communities and for communities in transition towards political community. *Mastery*, on the other hand, is primarily for the benefit of the master, although it provides the basic requirements of sustenance and security for the servant. It is not anticipated that the servant will participate seriously in planning and decision-making. Shades of this relationship are found today in the relationship between employer and employee.

When mastery is exercised in the political community, it is called *despotism* and is one of the failures in political life. It is actually a failure to achieve political life because it is in a sense pre-political. Since it does not respect the freedom, intelligence and capability of those who are ruled, it does not qualify as political rule. The difference can be seen in the difficulty often experienced by those who move from business to politics. A politician has to build consensus among all participants before acting, and this often takes time and much talking. A business executive moves more quickly to action and expects that people will do as they have been directed. Business leaders expect efficiency, but they often have difficulty recognising and dealing with the capacities of intelligent employees.

Despots can be benign, malign or enlightened. It is not uncommon for communities to hand despotic power to rulers who are benign and who have achieved a great deal of material good for the community. As a young businesswoman once said to me in French Polynesia, 'It is all very well to drink the milk of Mother France, but we want to be adults'. French Polynesians have lived with better facilities and services than most Pacific countries because of the resources allocated to them by France, but as they have been educated and their capabilities have increased, so has the desire to have a real place in decision-making about their futures.

The differences between mastery and political rule, and monarchy and other forms of rule, show why the political community or country is not just one homogeneous community but rather a large community composed of a number of smaller communities. Other kinds of social aggregations can also be important. The political art is to know how to find ways in which these different communities and the persons in them will be able to participate fully and fruitfully in the political life of their country.

Excursion One
Melanesia: The *Wantok* System

The terms *'wantok'* and *'wantok* system' occur surprisingly infrequently in the academic literature. When they do occur, they are often used in parentheses and with reference to difficulties experienced in Papua New Guinea (PNG), Solomon Islands and Vanuatu, such as failures of development projects or corruption in government. In common speech, however, the terms are ubiquitous and display a wide range of meanings and elicit a wide range of feelings. A *wantok*, literally 'one talk', in *Tok Pisin*, the most widely spoken official language of PNG, is the speaker of a common first or indigenous language and so is a relative, friend or neighbour in a manner that encompasses communal culture and kinship. The *wantok* system is a network of relationships and obligations, which we will explore shortly. A question frequently asked in response to discussions about political or economic development in PNG or Melanesia generally is: 'What about the *wantok* system?' This excursion will explore these meanings and feelings and attempt to understand the *wantok* system, its place in Melanesian life, its value, the problems it causes, and how we might answer the question, what about the *wantok* system?

Wantok in Popular Discourse

One way to explore popular perceptions is through the press and here we will survey some of the uses of *wantok* in the Papua New Guinea newspaper, the *Post-Courier*. It is used with warmth of feeling: 'I was privileged to spend the night with my good *wantok* . . . and his wife at their house' (3 December 2004). Pride is also expressed:

'PNG's *wantok* system is one of the most vibrant customary social support systems operating worldwide' (8 April 2008). Particularly telling are the expanded uses of the term. It enters into the names of sporting teams such as the Mendi *Wantok* Off-Cuts (27 March 2012) and of businesses such as Highlands *Wantok* Supermarket (5 March 2013). Commercial interests attempt to package their products in a friendly manner: *wantok moni* is a way of transferring money using a mobile phone (6 June 2013), and '*wantok* fares' are offered by Air Niugini (5 February 2007).

There is also ambivalence, as was expressed in an article on 5 June 2012:

> Papua New Guinea's *wantok* system can be a blessing and a curse. And this is where the problem lies. Many critics and detractors of the *wantok* system argue that it is the biggest obstacle to development, change and progress in Papua New Guinea and is probably one of the underlying reasons for corruption that is eating away at the heart of our society today. This may be true, but one thing is certain. The *wantok* system that we have today has been tried and tested down the centuries and is the foundation on which more than 800 unique cultures and more than one thousand tribes stand.

The writer is clearly torn between adherence to a cultural system that is and has been for so long fundamental to the lives of so many people, and the difficulties that it causes in a time of change, difficulties that include disruption of attempts at development of the country as a whole. In the writer's words, it is a blessing and a curse at the deepest levels.

Complaints against the effects of the *wantok* system are frequent. Many equate it with *nepotism*, which occurs when someone in authority gives a position or privileges to a clan member rather than to a more competent or deserving person. This makes it difficult, for instance, for people with otherwise good qualifications to find employment (24 June 2010) and conversely corrupts the businesses or government agencies that employ less than capable people (30 March 2006; 9 March 2010). Within organisations bonds and reciprocal obligations between members of the organisation can also divert it from its purposes. Complaints are made about the Royal Papua New Guinea Constabulary's ability to discharge its constitutional duty (16 August 2005), about incapacity in the Defence Force (31 December 2012) and about 'prison escapees roaming freely around the country' because of protection by their *wantoks* (7 December 2012). Problems internal to the *wantok* system are also raised: people given to gambling knowing that their *wantoks* will support them (5 January 2012); women abused by their husbands without the protection of the law (10 July 2009); movement of people into settlements without land or work because their *wantoks* are there (28 February 2013); acceptance of inappropriate medicine from a *wantok* rather than going to a doctor (11 April 2008). At the political level, we hear that 'people are not electing the best person during national elections. [They] vote for their *hausline*, *tambu* or *wantok* and this habit is alive and well' (2 November 2006).

Some writers show insight into what is happening and why the complaints arise. An economy based on money changes the way that people can reciprocate (14 January 2009) and life in urban areas among different peoples and with a cash-based economy puts the *wantok* system under stress (8 June 2012). Paul Barker put it in different terms:

> While the public demands the provision of the best staff and services, under the prevailing system of patronage leaders appoint *wantoks* and mates to key positions in exchange for support. Some politicians blame the community and custom for pressuring them, but this is a cop-out. A modern state cannot function on personal favours and obligations, but requires firm policies, procedures and standards, followed transparently. (17 July 2009)

The issue here is change and, in fact, momentous change. A system that worked well for small closed communities living in tightly defined geographical areas is challenged when it is drawn into a developing political system that embraces many peoples and that has to deal with imported ideas, technologies and economies.

What might be the solution? Some call for ethical standards (13 May 2013) and for appointments on merit (9 May 2013). A rule at Port Moresby General Hospital states that there is 'no entertainment of the *wantok* system' (12 June 2013). One writer in the *Post-Courier* had a broader suggestion:

> The concept of *wantoks* needs to be extended, to broadly encompass the idea of Papua New Guineans being an actual united race of people. All Papua New Guineans must consider themselves part of one great *wantok* race. This is not such a hard thing to do. Whenever a Papua New Guinean sees a fellow countryman overseas they recognise and greet each other first and foremost as Papua New Guineans. They know that, in the wider world, their tribal origin matters much less than the fact that they are from the same country. They are both essentially *wantoks* regardless of what tribe either may originally come from. When the Kumuls played against the Junior Kangaroos recently in Port Moresby, there were no Engans in the crowd, there were no New Irelanders, no Taris, no Papuans nor Sepiks. There were only Papua New Guineans urging on the Papua New Guinean team. (15 November 2005)

These discussions and many like them carry a great amount of wisdom. The *wantok* system is deeply entrenched in Papua New Guinean culture and will not go away. It gives people a sense of belonging to a community and the obligation of reciprocity ensures that people are looked after. It does, however, create difficulties when it is joined to modern systems of governance and organisation. During the remainder of this excursion we will rely on the academic literature to examine these issues and look at possible ways forward. This is not to say that a solution to the tensions will be easy or come quickly, because the change being experienced by Melanesian peoples is enormous. Especially in the case of PNG, it is complicated by a large population of extraordinary diversity and by geographical obstacles. We should, however, appreciate the large volume of intelligent discussion that is going on at the popular level.

What Is the *Wantok* System?

The term *wantok* arose in colonial times, when Papua New Guinea indigenes found themselves working on plantations away from their families and traditional lands. A communal people, they sought others with whom they could relate and on whom they could rely. Where possible, these were people who spoke the same language as they, although they lived in a land of some 830 languages. Ideally, they were kin or from the same clan or tribe. The *wantok* system, therefore, has its roots both in pre-colonial kinship systems and in the increasing disruption to traditional life brought by European contact. Prior to contact, kinship groups tended to be small and geographically isolated from their neighbours. People were divided into kinsfolk and strangers.[1] Although trade was practised, groups were largely self-sufficient and depended on subsistence farming. Kinship systems varied greatly across New Guinea and the islands of Melanesia, but it was generally common to them that members were related by marriage and descent and that reciprocity and the giving of gifts were critical dimensions of the cultures. In colonial and post-colonial times, movement of peoples has meant that the range of a person's significant relationships has grown to include not just kin but also people from the same language group, from the same geographical area and, more recently, from the same religion, the same province or from the whole country.[2] The term *wantok* is what philosophers call an *analogous concept*. It begins with a core or original meaning and extends, maintaining that core meaning but also allowing difference.

The wantok system is a set of arrangements that defines who is in a particular group and that organises how the members of that group relate to one another. The relationships are personal and built on affection. Respect is a significant virtue. Reciprocity—the giving and receiving of gifts—is central to the morality of the group, so that most transactions of goods are more than simply

1. See H Ian Hogbin, *Kinship and Marriage in a New Guinea Village* (London: Athlone Press, 1963), 13 ff. Literature abounds on kinship systems. See, for instance, Ronald M Berndt, *Excess and Restraint: Social Control Among a New Guinea Mountain People* (Chicago: University of Chicago Press, 1962). See also Andrew Strathern and Pamela J Stewart, *Kinship in Action: Self and Group* (New York: Prentice Hall, 2011). For a helpful article on how to negotiate kinship relationships, see R Daniel Shaw, 'Understanding Kinship and Social Structure', *Catalyst* 10/2 (1980): 92–104.
2. See Sinclair Dinnen, *Law and Order in a Weak State: Crime and Politics in Papua New Guinea* (Honolulu: University of Hawai'i Press, 2001), 11–16.

commercial. There may be calculation of value, but the exchange is more significant for the relationship it sustains. The arrangements are set in custom (*kastom*) rather than legislation and groups are generally led by a *bigman*, who has demonstrated ability in managing relationships and generosity in caring for the group and seeing to its external relationships. Solomon Islander, Gordon Leua Nanau, summarises in this way:

> The '*wantok* system' is a way of organising a society for subsistence living that ensures the survival of a group of people. It emphasises reciprocal networks and caring for each other's needs as and when necessary and ensures the security of members from external forces and threats.[3]

The *wantok* system, therefore, provides safe relationships so that people can, for instance, move from their village of origin to the city and be assured of accommodation, basic sustenance and company. Reciprocity ensures that those living in the city do not lose touch with their village and are able to return. Communities can function well and care for persons even under difficult circumstances, although they do have their limits and failure to reciprocate can lead to gradual exclusion.[4] Nevertheless, at times, the obligation to reciprocate can strain the recipient's limited pool of resources.

From the Aristotelian point of view, a *wantok* group is a pre-political community. It is this rather than a political community for two important reasons. First, because life is governed by *kastom*, it does not imagine that its rules can change. In fact, *kastom* does change but only either slowly over an extended time or more

---

3. Gordon Leua Nanau, 'The *Wantok System* as a Socio-Economic and Political Network in Melanesia', *OMNES: The Journal of Multicultural Society* 2/1 (2011): 31–51, at 35.
4. See Michael Monsell-Davis, 'Urban Exchange: Safety-Net or Disincentive?: *Wantoks* and Relatives in the Urban Pacific', *Canberra Anthropology* 16/2 (1993): 45–66. Monsell-Davis also compares the *wantok* system to the Fijian *kerekere* system. See also Michael Goddard, 'From Rolling Thunder to Reggae: Imagining Squatter Settlements in Papua New Guinea', *Contemporary Pacific* 13/1 (Spring 2001): 1–32. See also Emma Gilberthorpe, 'Fasu Solidarity: A Case Study of Kin Networks, Land Tenure and Oil', *American Anthropologist* 109/1 (March 2007): 1–112, at 1.

quickly in response to generally external threats, pressures or opportunities. This does not mean that *wantoks* do not engage in 'politics', but rather that they are not engaged in thoughtfully and constantly amending their laws and customs in search of better arrangements. Secondly, at least in its primary form, members are kin rather than people who are different. Nevertheless, as we have seen in earlier chapters, Aristotle builds his political community out of existing pre-political communities and he sees the *polis* or country as bound together by affection or friendship. In contrast, the Idea of the Modern State does away with pre-political communities so as to make the 'individual' the basic unit of the political community and imagines a state bound not by friendship but by fear in the form of the coercive powers of the state itself. Security and opportunity are found in the guise of rights and a state capable of enforcing them.[5]

Even, therefore, in the formation of a large and diverse country, the *wantok* system can be seen in a positive light. At present, most of the population of PNG live in rural areas away from cities and towns and at some distance from government. The *wantok* system underpins community order and tribal governance. It ensures systems of care and of restorative justice through village courts. It is the cultural energy that holds communities together. It is not unreasonable to hope that, as PNG forms as a nation, this same energy will generate a force for socio-political ordering.[6] The extension of the term that we noted earlier need not just be a play on words. It can, rather, denote an extension of the deep communal relations that bind kinship groups to relations that bind the whole country. The political question is, how do you construct a constitution and institutions in a way that recognises the networks of relationships that are already working in the country?

---

5. This is not to say that fear is absent from traditional PNG life. Hostility of neighbours and the practice of sorcery have long been present. See Neville Bartle, *Death, Witchcraft and the Spirit World in the Highlands of New Guinea* (Goroka, PNG: Melanesian Institute, 2005) and Franco Zocca, *Sanguma in Paradise: Sorcery, Witchcraft and Christianity in Papua New Guinea* (Goroka, PNG: Melanesian Institute, 2009).
6. Suggested by Bal Kama in a private communication.

When Does the *Wantok* System Become Disruptive?

It is not surprising, on the other hand, that the *wantok* system is frequently regarded as disruptive in the face of modern development. This disruption, as we have seen, is born out of the dislocation that followed colonisation. In addition, as can be seen clearly in the case of PNG, the amount and rate of change that the people of Melanesia are undergoing is enormous, and change usually disrupts people's lives. Although Britain and Germany proclaimed protectorates over East New Guinea in 1884, it was not until the 1930s, when planes flew over New Guinea, that the outside world recognised that large populations lived in the Highlands, and it was not till the 1960s that the majority of these people experienced contact with government officers (*kiaps*). If we recognise that the world as a whole has had difficulty coping with the rate of technological, social, economic and political change, the challenge to PNG is made clear. It is made more difficult not just by ethnic diversity but by the fact that the different regions—Papua, Momase, New Guinea Islands and the Highlands—have had different experiences along different time lines. There are, however, deeper reasons.

PNG became an independent country in 1975, Solomon Islands in 1978 and Vanuatu in 1980, which in the current world political system meant that they became sovereign states recognised by the United Nations and took on the form and structure of the modern *state*, also called the *nation-state*. The claim to be such a state implies certain assumptions. First, it assumes a *nation*, that is, a single people who are culturally and ethnically one and who recognise themselves as such so as to be able to live together peacefully. Secondly, it assumes an array of institutions in which officials act strictly in accord with their function and the rules surrounding it rather than in accord with personal allegiances and motives or in hope of gain. The most important of these institutions are the legislature or parliament, composed of democratically elected politicians usually belonging to ideologically formed parties; the government, composed of ministers and officials in the bureaucracy; and the judiciary, which is independent of both parliament and government and impartial towards those whom it judges. Thirdly, it presupposes a large economy that generates financial surpluses sufficient to run the apparatus of government and to allow the government to provide a wide range of services, particularly in education, health, transport, communications and security.

Left unchecked, the *wantok* system has the potential to disrupt all of these assumptions.[7] If *wantok* groups in Melanesian nations are too strong and too singular in their commitment to their own group to the exclusion of others, how can a nation be formed?[8] At the level of state institutions, Melanesia has an unfortunate legacy from colonial times in which many view the state as a source of material goods, that is, as a kind of patron, rather than as an institution in which all participate, so that political actors work constructively for the good of the whole.[9]

Indeed, the *wantok* system has shown that it is able to subvert most institutions. Politicians are often accused of showering beer or other goods on small parts of an electorate, generally *wantoks*, in order to gain power and get access to government 'slush funds'. Public servants may feel pressured to give preference to their *wantoks* rather than to strictly follow law and policy. Finally, judges and magistrates are often pressured by their *wantoks*, or are perceived to favour them. PNG, in particular, has great natural

7. John Connell, *Papua New Guinea: The Struggle for Development* (London: Routledge, 1997), covers a broad spectrum of the problems confronting development in PNG.
8. See, for instance, Anton Ploeg, 'Cultural Politics among the Siassi, Morobe Province, Papua New Guinea', *Bijdragen tot de Taal-en Volkenkunde* 149/4 (1993): 768–80. David Akin, 'Compensation and the Melanesian State: Why the Kwaio Keep Claiming', *Contemporary Pacific* 11/1 (Spring 1999): 35–67, explores the rather strong resistance of the Kwaio people of Malaita in the Solomon Islands to integration into a nation or even to recognition of the national government.
9. See Laurence Goldman, ' "Hoo–Ha in Huli": Considerations on Commotion and Community in the Southern Highlands', in *Conflict and Resource Development in the Southern Highlands of New Guinea*, edited by Nicole Haley and Ronald J May (Canberra: ANU E Press, 2007), 69–88, at 85. See also Robert J Gordon and Mervyn J Meggitt, *Law and Order in the New Guinea Highlands: Encounters with the Enga* (published for University of Vermont by University Press of New England, 1985), especially chapter 6, 'The Politics of Spoils'.

resources, particularly in minerals, gas, oil and timber, and these are generating increasing revenues, but there are complaints that the money is not managed properly and services are diminishing across the country, and that this can be attributed to the failure of its institutions.[10]

A final word needs to be said about how the *wantok* system can disrupt local life. First, it can make it impossible to run a small business successfully. Any business, whether it is a shop, a piggery or a chicken farm, needs to gather sufficient money and resources to begin and then to protect its profits so as to replenish stock or resources that have been sold. If the *wantok* system intervenes so that those resources are taken up in the cycle of gift-giving, the business will collapse. Secondly, there are growing claims that the *wantok* system makes living in urban areas more difficult. Although it assists those who have recently arrived in a town and those who have experienced hardship, as cities develop people have to rely on the cash economy, and money that is easily let go is soon dissipated.[11]

---

10. See Sinclair Dinnen, 'In Weakness and Strength: State, Societies and Order in Papua New Guinea', in *Weak and Strong States in Asia-Pacific Societies*, edited by Peter Dauvergne (Sydney: Allen and Unwin, 1998), chapter 3, pages 38–59. Peter Larmour, 'Corruption and Governance in the South Pacific', *State, Society and Governance in Melanesia Discussion Paper* 1997/5, <http://ips.cap.anu.edu.au/ssgm/>, accessed 15 July 2013, gives a sensitive account of the issues around corruption and traditional practices such as gift-giving. His later paper, 'Evaluating International Action Against Corruption in the Pacific Islands', *State, Society and Governance in Melanesia Discussion Paper* 2007/1, <http://ips.cap.anu.edu.au/ssgm/>, accessed 15 July 2013, examines efforts to reduce corruption across the Pacific. Alfred Tivinarlik and Carolyn L Wanat, 'Leadership Styles of New Ireland High School Administrators: A Papua New Guinea Study', *Anthropology and Education Quarterly* 37/1 (March 2006): 1–20, study the efforts of school principals to balance modern administration and communal values. See also Jane Turnbull, 'Solomon Islands: Blending Traditional Power and Modern Structures in the State', *Public Administration and Development* 22/2 (May 2002): 191–201.

11. See, for instance, Masahiro Umerzaki and Ryutaro Ohtsuka, 'Adaptive Strategies of Highlands: Origin Migrant Settlers in Port Moresby, Papua New Guinea', *Human Ecology* 31/1 (March 2003): 3–25. For other experiences, see Keith Barber, 'The Bugiau Community at Eight-Mile: An Urban Settlement in Port Moresby, Papua New Guinea', *Oceania* 73/4 (June 2003): 287–97; and Benedict Y Imbun, 'Mining Workers or "Opportunist" Tribesmen?: A Tribal Workforce in a Papua New Guinea Mine', *Oceania* 71/2 (December 2000): 129–49.

How Might *Kastom* and Modernity Meet?

There is growing recognition among researchers that the modern state in its standard forms may not suit countries such as those in Melanesia. Rod Nixon puts it this way:

> How realistic is it to superimpose the structure of the modern state indiscriminately, and expect in every instance that societies will reform their social and administrative systems in accordance with the model, even when this contradicts the momentum of their own economic and cultural realities?[12]

Similarly, Sinclair Dinnen declares:

> Contrary to much of the prevailing policy discourse, international state-building is not simply a technical exercise of capacity-development, but also raises important issues of politics and legitimacy.[13]

Questions are also raised about whether people want the kind of development they are being offered.[14] The frequently asked question, however, is: 'What about the *wantok* system?' We will conclude this excursion with three suggestions from the academic literature and a couple of common-sense observations.

The first suggestion is that Papua New Guineans, Solomon Islanders and ni-Vanuatu continue to build linkages between one another that go beyond their own immediate groups. We saw in the quotations from the *Post-Courier* that this is happening in Papua New Guinea, and in our analysis of the term, *wantok*, we saw that it is used analogously, extending possibly to the whole country. The meaning of the term is extended, but it can still carry a sense

---

12. Rod Nixon, 'The Crisis of Governance in New Subsistence States', *Journal of Contemporary Asia* 36/1 (2006): 75–101, at 81.
13. Sinclair Dinnen, 'State-Building in a Post-Colonial Society: The Case of the Solomon Islands', *Chicago Journal of International Law* 9/1 (Summer 2008): 51–78, at 52.
14. For a sensitive account, see Maev O'Collins, 'What If They Don't Want Your Kind of Development? Reflections on the Southern Highlands', in *Conflict and Resource Development in the Southern Highlands of Papua New Guinea*, edited by Nicole Haley and Ronald J May (Canberra: ANU E Press, 2007), 135–48.

of connectedness and affection. We might call this *nation-building*, and there is evidence that it is happening.[15] The *wantok* system has the potential to provide the cultural energy for this growth. Much of the change is occurring by means of smaller groups, such as regional associations, churches and sporting clubs, which develop linkages among people who previously saw themselves as very different. 'These ongoing developments are part of organic processes contributing to the emergence of new groupings and identities beyond traditional local ones. They include a slowly developing sense of national identity.'[16]

The second suggestion is that Papua New Guineans and the neighbouring Melanesian nations themselves develop and articulate properly national ethical positions. There is reason to suggest that the public ethical language of human rights does not fit well with Melanesian values and that in any case there may not be the means to enforce these rights.[17] Collaborative efforts between Melanesian scholars and various communities could 'help define ethical standards, based on ideas of what the "good life" is, how it is attained, and how it may be destroyed; how people should conduct themselves in business; how wealth should be distributed; how the family (in the extended sense) should be included in the running of business; and so on'.[18] What are the qualities of character that will allow Melanesian life in its changing circumstances to flourish? It is not romanticism to suggest that Melanesians have the resources in their culture, religion and

---

15. See Simon Feeny, Michael Leach and James Scambary, 'Measuring Attitudes to National Identity and Nation-Building in Papua New Guinea', *Political Science* 64 (2012): 121–44.

16. Anthony Regan, 'Clever People Solving Difficult Problems: Perspectives on Weakness of State and Nation in Papua New Guinea', *State Society and Governance in Melanesia Working Paper* 2005/2, <http://ips.cap.anu.edu.au/ssgm/>, accessed 15 July 2013.

17. See Onora O'Neill, 'Agents of Justice', *Metaphilosophy* 32/1–2 (January 2001): 180–95.

18. Elise Huffer, 'Governance, Corruption, and Ethics in the Pacific', *Contemporary Pacific* 17/1 (2005): 118–40, at 132.

experience to answer these questions.[19] In fact, Bernard Narakobi began articulating these ideas for PNG in the 1970s.[20]

The third suggestion is that researchers and professionals should work on culturally effective technical solutions to institutional problems. In 2005, Abraham Hauriasi and Howard Davey studied accounting in Solomon Islands.[21] They concluded that:

> Core indigenous values are increasingly threatened by the integration of the Solomon Islands into the global economy and the dominance of narrow economic values. It is important to highlight how compatible or otherwise these western values are with these indigenous values and to consider how these conflicting values could be adapted to engender positive outcomes.[22]

They drew up a series of proposals for how both accounting practices and Solomon Islands culture might adapt to achieve satisfactory outcomes.

A good deal can also be learnt from common sense and from shared experience, as we saw in the excerpts from the *Post-Courier* in the first section of this excursion. Two points will be sufficient here. First, all people learn to live in more than one community and 'system', whether they be families, clubs, workplaces or sporting teams. Each of these groups have different rules and people know what they are and are able to act rightly at the right time. Where a tightly defined *wantok* system has dominated, balance needs to be asserted by the other 'systems'. People need to attend to the system they are working in at the moment and to follow its rules. We saw this functioning in the hospital notice—'no entertainment of the *wantok* system'.

---

19. Ako Arua and Daniel Joh Eka, 'Wantok System', *Melanesian Journal of Theology* 18/1 (2002): 6–17, attempt to do just this.
20. See, for instance, Bernard Narakobi, *The Melanesian Way* (Boroko, PNG: Institute of Papua New Guinea Studies and Suva: Institute of Pacific Studies, 1980).
21. Abraham Haurisi and Howard Davey, 'Accounting and Culture: The Case of Solomon Islands', *Pacific Accounting Review* 21/2 (2009): 228–59, available at <www.emeraldinsight.com/0114-0582.htm>.
22. Haurisi and Davey, 'Accounting and Culture', 252.

Secondly, Papua New Guineans and their Melanesian neighbours would be wise to look around and see where local solutions have been tried and tested. If a businessman has found a way in which to separate money and resources that are his to share with his *wantoks* from money and resources that belong to the *bisnis* and so are not to be shared, this may demonstrate a technique that can be used by others. Government officials have put signs on their office doors saying, 'No *wantoks* allowed'.[23] Papua New Guineans, Solomon Islanders and ni-Vanuatu could also look more broadly to solutions found by Polynesians and Micronesians, who have confronted similar problems but who live in smaller and less complex countries.

---

23. Michael Kouro, who is remembered in the dedication of this book, was proud of such a notice on his office door when he was Public Solicitor.

Chapter Three
Learning from Experience

In Book II of the *Politics*, Aristotle begins again. Book I had looked at the natural origins of political community—pre-political communities, human nature and human need. In Book II he studies both what other writers have said about forming communities and the arrangements and the formation of actual political communities or countries. He justifies the first by suggesting that actual cities can perform better or worse, so that there is much to learn from those who have engaged in serious study. The examination of actual communities is important because here it is that we get ideas about how different peoples at different times have solved the problems involved in forming political communities. At a deeper level, this method recognises that political communities arise not just out of natural need but through thought and through action guided by practical judgement, and so experience is important. In this chapter, we will touch on some of the more critical points that Aristotle makes, because these begin to form the parameters of our thinking about politics. We will also make a brief foray into modern political forms. Before we do this, however, there are two fundamental points that can now be made clear.

First, Aristotle begins, 'it is our intention to study the sort of political [community] that is superior to all for those capable of living as far as possible in the manner one would pray for'.[1] Aristotle is searching for the best—the best kind of political arrangement and the best kind of life. Each of these will remain important themes throughout our study, but it will be helpful to expand on the best kind of political arrangement now. In Book IV, Aristotle clarifies four

---

1. Aristotle, *Politics* II, 1 (1260b28), 55, substituting 'community' for 'partnership'.

different senses of the best arrangements for constituting a political community. The first is the *best possible arrangement of all*, the one that we would pray for and that might in fact be realised, if circumstances were adequate and we did the right things. Though rarely achieved, it is not just an ideal but rather a guide to our thought about reasonable possibilities. The second is the *best possible arrangement that particular circumstances might allow*. The point is that individual countries are sometimes limited by things such as geography or natural resources, so that some accommodation needs to be made. The third is the *best possible arrangement that a particular people may be able to achieve*. Here we can imagine factors such as culture, history, capacity and past learning that put limits on and modify what is actually possible. An important factor here is the current political arrangement, because this is how the people have in fact learnt to live. Change requires new learning and may come slowly and in the face of resistance. The fourth is the *best practicable arrangement for most people in most places in most times*. Aristotle seems to think that, given time, good leadership and luck, most people could achieve it. Each of these senses of the best political arrangement will be at play during our investigation and each is helpful for thinking about what a country might do.[2]

The second fundamental point that Aristotle makes is that the central question of political theory has to do with how people are enabled to participate or to share in the life of the political community or country. In its broadest sense, this question has to do with how people live—the work they do, the common activities that they share with others, the virtues that enable them to function well and ultimately the kind of education they need to live this way. In its narrower sense, the question has to do with those activities specific to the political community itself—decision-making, judging, passing laws, exercising office, ensuring order, electing officials and so on. It is clear that not everyone can do the same thing at the same time, but how are these activities to be shared around? How are they to be distributed in a way that will seem fair to everybody? How are they to be distributed in a way that ensures that the country functions effectively? These are the questions that concern us.

---

2. Aristotle, *Politics* IV, 1 (1288b20–40), 118.

Aristotle's Criticism of Other Writers

In Book II, most of Aristotle's analysis and criticism is directed towards Plato's work, the *Republic*, which was one of the most significant writings of Aristotle's time. It does not mean that he is in substantial disagreement with his teacher, Plato, because Plato wrote his dialogues in order to test ideas and to challenge people to think. This is illustrated by Aristotle's agreement with most of what is said in Plato's other work, the *Laws*, although even here he indicates minor disagreements. It is Socrates who speaks in each of the dialogues, though the positions he espouses in each are quite different. Aristotle finally argues briefly with two other authors, Phaleas of Chalcedon and Hippodamus of Miletus, who allow him to make some strategic points. We will not follow the detail of the arguments but rather see some of the main conclusions that Aristotle reaches.

In the *Republic*, Socrates searches for the perfect country, in which justice will always prevail. Expecting perfect unity in the country, he proposes that women, children and property be held in common, so that there are no discernible differences among people—all are related to all and everyone can feel ownership for the whole. In some ways, the ideas are similar to thoughts put forward by modern communism. Aristotle's objections raise three major points.

First, although a country must in some sense be a unity, there are different kinds of unity. That of the country is not the kind of unity that Socrates is seeking. A *country* is composed of a multitude of people who differ in kind. A country seeks to be more self-sufficient than a household or a village, and so it draws together people of different skills and capacities in order that together they may be able to supply the various needs of the whole country. Aristotle draws a distinction between an *alliance*, in which different communities join together simply to be quantitatively greater for things such as defence, and a *country*, which needs to be large enough to have the range of skills and resources necessary for self-sufficiency. This is a qualitative increase and involves people who have different capacities and interests. A country does, nevertheless, need to be a unity and Aristotle later points out that this will come through education, as everyone learns to live with the same laws, developing similar habits, and achieving common understandings.[3] Today we might speak about being a nation or achieving a single identity.

The Solomon Islands presents an interesting case. It is composed of nine provinces at the core of which are six large islands. In former times, these islands were far enough apart for the inhabitants to live quite separate lives and so to develop different ways and cultures. Now, with fast transport and communications, their proximity and size invite them to form one country. In what sense are the Solomon Islands one—by accidents of geography and history; by an alliance seeking greater size; by becoming one political community in which differences are recognised and seen to contribute to self-sufficiency and richness of life in one country? It would seem that in some respects a single identity is emerging but in a process that will take considerable time to reach its fulfilment.

A different kind of situation is found between Guam and the Commonwealth of the Northern Mariana Islands (CNMI). Geographically they form one line of islands that are reasonably close to one another. In pre-contact times, the Chamorro people moved easily between the islands, of which Guam is the largest and southernmost. However, a separation occurred at the end of the nineteenth century when Spain sold Guam to the United States and the other islands to Germany. Although both are now part of the United States—CNMI as a commonwealth and Guam as unincorporated territory of the United States—attempts to unite them into one political community have failed. It is fair to ask whether the two might draw further apart due to growing differences in the composition of the population, to differences in their economies and to differences in their communal experience.

Aristotle's second objection to Plato's proposal that women, children and property be held in common is that, if all the adults in a community were to say of all the children that they are 'mine', considerable confusion would arise. The sense in which one could speak of 'my children' would become greatly diluted. On a more positive note, Aristotle recognises that love and affection are among the greatest human goods and that these occur most commonly and most richly between husbands and wives, between parents and children and between wider kin who live with and respect one another.

---

3.   Aristotle, *Politics* II, 5 (1263b35), 62.

This is good for the country as well, because Aristotle says many times that it is affection and friendship that binds a country. The contrary is also relevant. Where people live closely together without love and respect, disagreements will boil over into violence and murder, and desire will lead to licentiousness and depravity. Those who are weak will be preyed upon.

Thirdly, Aristotle disagrees with Socrates on the ownership of property. If land and crops were all owned in common, resentment would break out, even if, as Socrates proposes, meals were held in communal halls. There is a wide variety of ways in which various forms of property can be owned and distributed. Aristotle suggests that under the best arrangements 'everyone has his own possessions, but makes some of them useful to his friends, and some he uses as common things'.[4] He distinguishes between ownership and use and recognises that each must contribute to the country as a whole, whether this is done through taxation or some other contribution.

Aristotle gives two arguments for private ownership. The first is that people care for things that are their own, whereas things owned in common are usually neglected. The second is that there is pleasure associated both with the ownership of things and with the ability to give to others. This is the sense in which he sees the use of property as common. One should share generously with family, friends and neighbours. He sees this as more virtuous than someone who greedily accumulates everything for himself. In his discussion of the *Laws*, he suggests that one should have sufficient property to live 'with moderation and liberally', so that one neither indulges in luxury nor lives in hardship.[5]

In criticising the second author, Phaleas, Aristotle focuses on his proposal that every citizen should own an equal amount of property. The purpose of this proposal is that it would make everybody equal and hence ensure both peace and participation in the life of the community. While he can see reasons for limiting property, Aristotle finds this mechanism too simple and too materialistic to work. People come into conflict not just over property and other necessary things but over honours and even trivial things. Besides, it is human desire that needs to be controlled, because in human beings who are

---

4. Aristotle, *Politics* II, 5 (1263a34), 61.
5. Aristotle, *Politics* II, 6 (1265a33), 65.

indulgent desire grows and becomes insatiable. Control of desire is achieved through education and upbringing. Aristotle points out that there are many kinds of wealth and that differences of merit among people lead them to expect difference in what they possess. So, Aristotle's conclusion is that, at root, Phaleas' solution is too simple to work.

Property is a significant issue in many Pacific countries, in which most land is held under customary law and title, and so cannot be sold. Tension arises in relation to the ways of the modern economic world, in which land is regarded as a commodity, which can be bought, sold and mortgaged, and in which individual title is very strong. Many people, including Australian Aboriginal peoples, find this alienating. Aristotle would probably be more in favour of customary ways, which ensure that the whole community benefits. Nevertheless, the issues are complex and deserve study in their own right. In times of change, comparison of practices and experiences in different countries can be helpful in finding new ways. We will return to this topic in Chapter Nine.

The third person whose thought Aristotle analyses is Hippodamus. His proposals are not so simple. To start with, he divides things into threes—three kinds of people (artisans, farmers and soldiers); three uses of territory (sacred, public for warriors and private for farmers); three kinds of law (against arrogant behaviour, injury and death). Aristotle makes two criticisms of Hippodamus that are helpful for us. First, his proposal is too technical. Hippodamus relies on mathematics and takes no account of differences in the people or of the relationships among them or of the conditions of the land, whereas arrangements should be worked out practically and according to the conditions that prevail in the country, not by remote and abstract thought. Today we would call Hippodamus a *rationalist*. Secondly, Aristotle objects to one of Hippodamus' laws, which offers a reward to anyone who invents a new law. While Aristotle acknowledges that laws need to change as conditions change so as not to become meaningless, this ought not to happen just at whim but slowly and carefully. People obey laws through the habits that they develop from living under them, and those habits need time to form. Rapid and novel changes will simply weaken the law. When lawmakers have too strong a desire for innovation and change, they tend to bring about 'change for change's sake', which leaves people confused and unsettled.

The Modern State

At this point, it will be helpful if we leave Aristotle for a moment and take note of modern political theory, because it is this that continues to have a major impact on political thinking in the West and around the world as a whole. What we are confronting here is the Idea or theory of the Modern State, articulated most clearly by Thomas Hobbes (1588–1679) in his *Leviathan*, softened and modified by John Locke (1632–1704) in his *Second Treatise on Government*, and idealised as the final stage of human political development by GWF Hegel (1770–1831) in his *Elements of the Philosophy of Right*. I want to distinguish between what I will term the Idea of the Modern State and the Modern European State. The *Idea of the Modern State* is a product of the thought of philosophers, but it is intricately entwined with the historical development of the *Modern European State*, which is a political form that developed in Europe during the last four hundred years and is now found in most European and Western countries. Although it occurs with significant variation, it is seen as a model for all countries by many of those who wield influence on the contemporary world stage. We have already noted the difficulty that this model has for small Pacific states, but for now we will stay with the Idea of the Modern State, particularly as it was proposed by Hobbes.

Hobbes' account of the origins of political life is very different from and in direct opposition to that of Aristotle. He begins not with pre-political communities but with isolated individuals living in a condition of 'war of all against all', in which life is 'solitary, poor, nasty, brutish and short'.[6] Seeking peace and comfort, these individuals contract together to form a *commonwealth* by installing a *sovereign* (whether an individual or an assembly), who will enjoy absolute power and ensure internal peace by keeping the people in sufficient fear of retribution to dissuade them from conflict with one another. The power of the sovereign is absolute, and the sovereign can do no

---

6. Thomas Hobbes, *Leviathan*, edited by JCA Gaskin (Oxford: Oxford University Press, 1998), chapter 13, numbers 8 and 9, page 84.

wrong apart from abandoning the citizens to attack by outside forces. According to Hobbes, his theory is final, and once the sovereign or Leviathan (a biblical monster) is installed there is no place for further political thought and judgement.

There is much in this theory to which we might object. The obliteration of prepolitical communities, particularly families and clans but also of groups working within a country, supposes a much more solitary world than that described by Aristotle. The absolute power of the sovereign or what we have come to call the state led to dreadful regimes in the twentieth century such as those under Hitler and Stalin. The idea that a community be fundamentally bound by fear of the state rather than by affection and friendship of one another suggests a very hostile world. That citizens are expected to be predominantly busy in economic activity generating comfort for themselves rather than engaging in thought about the nature of communal life itself and about the best ways in which they might organise themselves removes the truth-seeking aspect of human life. The sense that the Idea of the Modern State is thought to be a final political form accounts for the fact that Western powers and theorists tend to push a single form of statehood on all countries and peoples.

The term 'state', which was coined by Machiavelli and which in this book we will usually avoid, has two distinct but related meanings, both leaning on the notion of sovereignty. In the first, it is the bearer of sovereign power. It is somewhat abstract in the sense that it is not identical with those who are elected or appointed to rule, but rather stands silently behind them. It is also abstract in the sense that it is not identical with the whole political community, which we have called a country, or with the whole life of this community. This is mostly clearly developed in the thought of Locke, who excluded certain matters such as religion and certain areas of ethics from the interest of the state. He rejected neither religion nor ethics, but made them private matters so that people could have different religions and customs without coming into conflict. The state, he thought, should take interest in ethical matters only if particular actions brought harm to innocent persons. The political ideology arising from these views is called *liberal democracy*.

In the second major meaning of 'state', each state is sovereign in relation to other states. Historically, this grew out of the principle established in the Treaty of Westphalia (1648) that decreed that borders of states were stable and that no state had grounds to interfere in the affairs of other states. Although the principle has been challenged in recent decades, it remains central to the current international system and determines how states relate to one another and, indeed, how the United Nations works. A difficulty often faced by small states is that they have to work as states in this second sense, but they may not have the capacity or desire to function as states in the first sense.

Analysis of Existing Countries

In the final chapters of the *Politics*, Book II, Aristotle considers the regimes that were operating in Sparta, Crete and Carthage, which were neighbours of Athens. He finds that the constitutions and laws of these countries are very similar, but he notices finer differences in law and practice and notes where these small differences affect life for better or worse. In examining different arrangements, Aristotle raises two questions. First, is a piece of legislation well done in respect of the best possible way of doing it? Secondly, is it in tune with how the country imagines itself and the kind of life proposed for the people? He equates the first question with the *happiness* of the city; the second question relates to the nature of the *constitution*. He offers a test for effective law. 'It is a sign of a well-organised constitution if the people voluntarily acquiesce in the arrangement of the constitution, and if there has never been factional conflict worth mentioning.'[7]

We will deal with just one of Aristotle's observations. He notes that Sparta is a warlike country and that legislators have proudly aimed to maintain this. They have, therefore, taken great pains to provide education and upbringing for men in order to make them strong, courageous and fierce. But they have neglected the upbringing of women, who have become licentious and given to luxury. One can imagine a country in which the men are often away at war but then come home with much loot and take to feasting and orgies. Aristotle points out that this situation makes people prize wealth, which then becomes concentrated in the hands of a few. As a result, Sparta's ability to maintain military force is weakened. He claims that this has

---

7.   Aristotle, *Politics* II, 11 (1272b30), 81, substituting 'constitution' for 'regime'.

been harmful both to the happiness of the city and to the intention of the constitution.

In the Pacific, a traveller can be surprised by the level of personal safety in Port Vila, Vanuatu. It is possible to walk safely around the city late at night, which contrasts with a high level of danger in places such as Port Moresby, in Papua New Guinea. On enquiry, one finds that Vanuatu solved the problem of city violence by bringing the chiefs of the various rural districts to town to appoint surrogate chiefs for the city. These meet regularly with the people from their own area, and if trouble breaks out, it is the city chiefs who are called rather than the police. The appointment of city chiefs has been successful both for the general happiness of the country and in respect of how it understands traditional forms of authority. Those in the city are no longer isolated from the relationships and customs of their rural communities. City life, though still different from village life, is no longer simply alien but is integrated into the life of the whole country.

The point of this final section is that an important part of the study of politics is to examine other countries both to see what has failed and to see what has worked. It is important to exchange the ideas and experiences of similar countries. Too often, Pacific island countries have received constitutions, laws and policy that might better suit their large neighbours. It is now time for them to learn from one another about how best to adapt the kind of life possible in their countries to a world in which global forces play an increasingly significant part. Getting the details of law right is difficult and depends on good practical judgement. That judgement is assisted by reflection on the successes and failures of others.

Chapter Four
The Life of the Citizen and Kinds of Constitution

In this chapter we will move more deeply into Aristotle's own understanding of the nature of a country or political community. We will follow sections of Books III and IV of the *Politics*. What is a *country*? In answering this question, Aristotle follows his usual method of identifying the elements or fundamental parts of a thing, then determining how they are arranged in relation to one another and finally investigating how the whole thing functions. In the case of the political community, the fundamental parts are the *citizens*; the arrangement is the *constitution*; and the manner of functioning is the division and working of the various institutions and offices of *government*. These will be the topics of this chapter. In so far as a political community is the outcome of human endeavour, there will not be one form for all communities, and so this first investigation will set out the broad range of possibilities.

Citizens and Country

Clearly, a *citizen* is a human being living in or connected to a particular place among people who are constituted as a single community. Yet, not every person living in a place is a citizen. Foreigners come and go and may become long-term residents. Children may be citizens, but in an incomplete way, because they do not participate in the political life of their country. As well, persons living in a place can be identified in other ways, for instance, as members of families, villages and towns. Other differences, such as means of livelihood and whether a person lives in rural areas or in the city, will become important but are not part of the definition of the citizen. Citizens participate in the life specific to their membership of a political community by participating in the formal and legal actions of the country, especially those involving deliberation and judgement, but also in things such as rituals. This gives Aristotle his formal definition of a citizen and a provisional definition of a country:

> Who the citizen is, then, is evident from these things. Whoever is entitled to participate in an office involving deliberation or decision is, we can now say, a citizen in this [country]; and the country is the multitude of such persons that is adequate with a view to self-sufficient life, to speak simply.[1]

There is, of course, another kind of definition, which we can term a legal definition, and which spells out who is entitled to participate in this way and so to call themselves citizens. A straightforward legal definition of a citizen is one who is born in a country to parents who are citizens. This is often insufficient, however, because people do move from country to country, marry, settle and work for the good of their new country. At some point, it seems just that they claim to be citizens. Events such as war may see a territory change hands and then it is necessary to find a manner of attributing citizenship that is fair.

The Pacific countries are interesting in this respect. Particularly in Polynesian and Micronesian countries there is a long history of movement of peoples. In parts, such as Fiji and Tonga and the Solomon Islands, there is an ancient history of war and conquest. No doubt, people found ways of accommodating these changes. The momentous change, however, was European contact, which led to most Pacific islands, apart from Tonga, becoming colonies of European powers and sometimes having a resident expatriate population. With independence and the formation of new states between 1960 and 1980, new legal definitions of citizens had to be established that took account of history, recognised the ethnic basis of the new countries and could be deemed just for all affected persons. In some places, such as Bougainville and Samoa, this was complicated by new state boundaries that did not conform either to local geography or to ancient allegiances. The division of much of

---

1.   Aristotle, *Politics* III, 1 (1275b16–20), 87, substituting 'country' for 'city'.

Micronesia into distinct countries owes more to colonial history than to traditional associations.

Aristotle raises a related question that brings to attention the sense in which a *country* is a unity and carries an identity. He asks whether after a country has gone through a profound change due to invasion or revolution the new country is liable for the debts of the old. This is equivalent to asking whether a newly independent country that was formerly a colony is liable for the debts of the former colonisers. Obviously, in these cases very fine points will be argued and strength will play a part, but Aristotle uses the example to show that a country is more than just territory and people. The definition of a political community includes people and land but it also includes the form that determines the kind of community it is and establishes it as a single identifiable community. We call this a *constitution*, and we will examine it in the next section.

Before leaving the discussion of the citizen, Aristotle asks an interesting question. Is the virtue of a good citizen identical with the virtue of a good person, as discussed in the *Ethics*? His answer is long and detailed and bears study in its own right, but briefly he concludes that in a well-formed country the good citizen will be a good person, but in a badly formed, deviant or misdirected country a good citizen will not necessarily be a good person. This draws attention to the virtue of the citizen, which is the preservation of the country, both by acting to make the country function well and by living the virtues that are properly identified as part of the life of the country. In a republic, an important virtue is the ability both 'to rule and to be ruled'. These are not the same, and so we need to learn to do both well.

Modern countries are very large, and so most citizens participate simply by voting in elections for representatives to parliaments. It is called *representative government*. How do we decide for whom we will vote? Often enough we probably decide on the basis of family loyalties, old friendships, allegiance to political parties, hope of benefit, or strong feelings about political issues. Aristotle suggests that we should be looking for the best person to carry the office and suggests three qualities: affection for the constitution of the country as it stands; a very great capacity for work; and virtue, both intellectual and moral, including a strong sense of justice.[2] He is clear that for a

---

2. Aristotle, *Politics* V, 9 (1309a33–5).

country to function well it needs both a good constitution and good office holders.

Possible Constitutions

Aristotle defines a *constitution* as 'an arrangement of a country with respect to its offices, particularly the one that has authority over all matters'.[3] Later he expands this definition:

> A constitution is an arrangement in [countries] connected with the offices, establishing the manner in which they have been distributed, what the authoritative element of the [constitution] is, and what the end of the [community] is in each case; and there are distinct laws among the things that are indicative of the [constitution]—those in accordance with which the rulers must rule and guard against those transgressing them.[4]

The development between these two definitions is interesting, because it shows how Aristotle works. In the early stages of his discussions, he is interested in the clearest and most formal distinctions and definitions. As these are clarified, however, he extends the scope of his discussion to include more detail and complexity.

This applies to his understanding of constitution. In the first sense, it is the distribution of offices and definition of the most authoritative body. Modern written constitutions are usually concerned mainly with the arrangement of offices and distribution of authority. Even this tells us much about a country, for instance, whether it is a democracy or a monarchy, and who controls what functions. In the second sense, however, Aristotle's understanding is much fuller and the constitution includes the arrangement of all parts and of various kinds of part in the country. It includes, for instance, how various towns and villages and even clans might relate to one another and to the whole. It includes how education and health services function

---

3. Aristotle, *Politics* III, 6 (1278b9), 94, substituting 'constitution' for 'regime' and 'country' for 'city'.
4. Aristotle, *Politics* IV, 1 (1289a14–18), 119, substituting 'constitution' for 'regime', 'country' for 'city' and 'community' for 'partnership'.

and how they are funded. This is a broader notion of constitution than we usually find in a modern constitution.

He adds another element in the second definition. Political communities are not formed out of sheer necessity, as might households or villages. Rather, as we saw in Chapter Two, human beings are 'political animals', who enjoy living together and who do so for reasons other than mere necessity, even if material advantages may flow from the larger community. This raises the question of the end or the good that communities seek. Even though the answer might be complex and often confused, we can point to countries that are focussed on war or on comfort or on religious practice or on sport or on learning or on higher cultural pursuits. These differences give a particular character to each of the communities. We will return to this topic in Chapters Five, Eight and Ten.

For now we can return to Aristotle's sparsest and most formal distinctions. Constitutions are distinguished by the nature of the rule of their most authoritative element. We have already seen that political rule is essentially different from household management or mastery of servants, because it is rule of those who are citizens and therefore participants in the life of the community. Aristotle further distinguishes constitutions that are *correct* or good in so far as the authoritative element rules for the sake of the whole community, and those that are *deviant* or bad because the rulers rule for their own advantage. A final distinction is between constitutions in which *one person rules*, constitutions in which *a small number of persons rule* and constitutions in which *everyone participates in governance*. This allows Aristotle to identify six formal kinds of constitution, which are best displayed in Table One below.

Once these formal distinctions are made, a much more involved discussion can take place, and Aristotle does this in Book IV, where he distinguishes different kinds of democracy, oligarchy and so on. For instance, a democracy in which everyone votes but only a few can stand for office is different from one in which everyone can both vote and stand for office. This discussion is detailed and useful because it shows that there can be much fine-tuning in a constitution and that it is this fine-tuning that makes a constitution successful. The goal is to identify the different parts of a community and to enable each to participate in ways that both do justice to them and allow the

community to function well. For now we will simply note three major
conclusions that Aristotle draws.

Table One. Forms of Constitution—The Formal Possibilities

	Correct Forms of Constitution
Kingship	Rule of one (monarchy), in which the king rules for the sake of the people.
Aristocracy	Rule of the few who are virtuous and for the sake of the people.
Republicanism	Rule of the multitude for the sake of the whole people.
	Deviant Forms of Constitution
Democracy	Rule of the multitude for self-advantage.
Oligarchy	Rule of the few for self-advantage.
Tyranny	Rule of one for self-advantage, and the most severe failure of political rule.

First, the most important division in a community is usually that
between *the wealthy* and *the poor*. The wealthy claim a right to rule
on the basis of their wealth; the poor claim a right to rule on the basis
of freedom. Because the wealthy are generally few in number and the
poor many, oligarchy tends to be rule by the wealthy and democracy
tends to be rule by the poor. The tension between these two groups is
in many ways the engine that drives political activity. For instance, in
Australia, of the major political parties, the Liberal Party has tended
to align with the wealthy and the Labor Party has tended to align
with the poor. In Melanesian countries, one sees a difference between
those who live in towns and cities and work for wages or salaries and
those who live in rural areas and grow their own food in a largely
subsistence economy. The third claim to rule is by *those who are
virtuous*, which would lead to aristocratic rule, although the finest
people often stay out of the political fray.

Secondly, a constitution is *never completely and purely one kind*
or another. One may name it in a certain way because its most
authoritative body works that way, but one will find that at other
levels, different forms of constitution are involved. For instance,
Australia calls itself a democratic country because all of its citizens
both vote and are eligible to stand for parliament, which is the most

authoritative body. Judges, however, are appointed aristocratically on the basis of merit both in skill at law and in personal integrity. One can imagine some of the difficulties that would arise if judges were elected democratically. In an extreme form of democracy, they would be selected by lot from among all citizens, which would more than likely lead to chaos. It is this blending of constitutional forms that allows those who help form the country to take account of the different capacities and claims of different members of the community and different groups within the community.

Thirdly, in each of the different constitutions, Aristotle notes a great difference between those in which *the law rules* and those in which *those in office rule*. We have come to call the first 'the rule of law'. According to the second, a minister or an assembly can simply decide on a course of action as they see fit at the moment. Aristotle points out several times that in the heat of the moment and under pressure, people will follow their emotions rather than reason coolly. Law, on the other hand, can generally be written with much thought and care, so that it acts dispassionately and is fair to all. We are all much more secure if we are able to live under the rule of law. Aristotle does allow an exception and it is commonly applied today. A judge or a minister of the government may be given discretion under the law to waive the law in particular cases, when a person is disadvantaged because of exceptional circumstances or circumstances that the written law could not foresee.

Political Institutions and Offices

The final questions of this chapter are about what there is to be shared under the constitution and how it will be divided. While ultimately these questions could be taken to include everything that is on offer in the country, including property and food, their first focus is on the decisions, judgements and actions of the country itself and on how access to these is distributed among citizens. This is because at the level of constitution, law and even policy, only so much can be achieved. Ultimately, successful outcomes are dependent on the right people making the right decisions at the right time. The skill of the constitutional planner or founder of a country is to design the various institutions and offices of the country and the ways in which they will be filled in such a way that all citizens will accept that they have been justly included and that the country will be able to act effectively.

Aristotle envisages three areas of function, which he calls the deliberative, the official and the judicial. In some respects, this looks like the modern division of legislature, executive and judiciary, but it is not quite the same. For Aristotle, the *deliberative* involves all the areas in which the citizens as a whole should have a say, which includes legislation, policy, some major decisions such as going to war, and judgements of a very serious nature. Aristotle also expects that in the small Greek *polis* all citizens could at times be present for deliberation about serious issues. This is not the case in the modern world, where communication technologies and transport tend to make our countries much larger. As has been already mentioned, we cope with this by *representative democracy*, according to which all citizens elect the more significant deliberative body. We also use referendums in cases involving major decisions, and general elections are held regularly and frequently.

Even in the modern division, there is room for difference, particularly in how the functions of legislating, determining policy and executing action are distributed. In the Westminster system developed first in the British Parliament, the leader of the larger party or coalition in the parliament is the effective head of the executive, so that questions of policy as well as legislation are often debated in the parliament. In the American presidential system, the executive is separate from the Congress, which is a law-making body, and the President forms the executive arm of government by choosing ministers who are not members of Congress. Congress does, however, assert itself in matters of policy and action by having to pass budget Bills and by processes of confirming the appointments of significant officials appointed by the President.

In Pacific countries, it is often asked whether the Westminster system and its derivatives suit the cultures of the people. Papua New Guinea, for instance, experienced years when the government was fairly unstable, because people in parliament would often shift allegiance from one party to another and vote against the government of the day in a no-confidence motion. Adjustments have been made to the constitution, such as a requirement that those elected in parties remain in those parties for a certain time, and other laws have been passed in an effort to rectify this situation. Bougainville, on the other hand, adopted a presidential system, which means that the executive would stay stable between elections and that the House of Representatives would engage in debate and establish law. There is potential in this arrangement for a House that will not always vote along strict party lines and even for one that might discuss serious matters at length until a reasonable consensus forms in a more traditional way.

Concerning the *official* or *executive* function, this today is divided between departments, which are run by permanent public servants. They are, however, presided over by members of government: in the Westminster system by ministers, who are elected members of parliament; in the American system by secretaries, appointed by the President. These ministers or secretaries carry real responsibility and authority. There are some departments that appear in every country and seem to be quite necessary, such as those dealing with revenue, expenditure, security, land, commerce, education and health. Going against modern practice, Aristotle here includes a department for 'superintendence . . . connected with sacred things' and maintenance of religious property. [5] Others, however, are put in place to deal with specific needs of the place and time. For instance, many countries have developed departments for the environment in recent decades and some are likely to have departments for climate change. Some Pacific countries have departments for women and children, because they recognise a need for special care for them. Aristotle notes that in small countries different functions may be placed together in a single department because there are fewer resources and personnel but also because the work is less than would be the case in a larger country. Pacific countries frequently do this, and the art is to arrange a satisfactory mix of responsibilities. Some functions, however, such as expenditure and auditing, should never both be in the hands of one official.

Judicial functions are divided among different courts. This allows courts to have different areas of expertise, and it enables superior courts to deal with only the more serious matters. Some courts deal with criminal matters, others with civil disputes between people and others with constitutional matters. Some Pacific countries have

---

5. Aristotle, *Politics* VI, 8 (1332b18), 195.

courts to deal with traditional land ownership and titles. There are generally courts of appeal, to which people can go if they believe that the judgement of a lower court was unfair. The authority of each of these courts needs to be established in law.

In the appointment of legislators, officials and judges, there are three determining questions—who appoints? who is eligible for appointment? and what is the manner of selection (vote, appointment, lottery)? These procedures will be more democratic if all citizens are involved; more oligarchic, if those with wealth and influence mostly are involved; and more aristocratic, if those with good education and character mostly are involved. At once, one can see that there are many ways in which offices can be distributed and that these affect the texture of the constitution. Some of these details will be determined directly by law, but sometimes they are affected indirectly by conditions specified by law. For instance, a legislature will be more democratic if legislators are paid and more oligarchic if they are not, because in the latter case only the wealthy will be able to afford to be elected. Similar influence can be exerted by making voting compulsory or voluntary. What we see, therefore, is that small items of law can affect the conditions under which people can act, and that this ultimately has an effect on the constitution.

Excursion Two
Fiji: A Long Crisis

That Fiji is constitutionally unsettled is obvious to anyone with even minimal acquaintance with the country and its history. The most obvious sign in recent decades has been a series of military coups between 1987 and 2006, numbered as four or six depending on how they are counted, but there are many other signs.[1] Since independence in 1970, Fiji has had four constitutions—its 1970 independence Constitution, which was an act of the British Parliament and grew out of the arrangements in place at the end of the colonial period as well as extended negotiations; its 1990 Constitution, which attempted to ensure supremacy of indigenous Fijians; its 1997 Constitution, which attempted to find a more moderate balance of the voices of both indigenous Fijians and Indo-Fijians; and its 2013 Constitution, which eliminated race-based electoral roles and quotas, electoral districts and the Council of Chiefs. Other events are also important: various labour strikes, particularly in the sugar industry; occasional violence, such as that which erupted around the 2000 coup; significant court judgements, such as that which restored the 1997 Constitution.[2]

---

1. Steven Ratuva, 'The Military Coups in Fiji: Reactive and Transformative Tendencies', *Asian Journal of Political Science* 19/1 (2011): 96–120, argues for six military coups. Stephen McCarthy, 'Soldiers, Chiefs and Church: Unstable Democracy in Fiji', *International Political Science Review* 32/5 (2011): 563–78, argues for four.
2. Two books provide detailed analysis of constitutional, electoral and military aspects of recent Fijian history. Jon Fraenkel and Stewart Firth, editors, *From Election to Coup in Fiji: The 2006 Campaign and Its Aftermath*, (Canberra: ANU E Press and Asia Pacific Press, 2007); Jon Fraenkel, Stewart Firth and Brij V Lal, *The 2006 Military Takeover in Fiji: A Coup to End All Coups?*, State Society

This state of affairs has serious consequences for the lives of citizens of the Fiji Islands. It brings immediate hardship for many in Fiji, who are not necessarily responsible for the difficulties but are dependent on a well-functioning country for employment and the opportunity to bring their children up well. It fosters tension and even conflict between citizens, who might otherwise live peacefully as neighbours but who are distanced from one another by the political divisions. It complicates relations with the rest of the world, and this in turn affects the economy and limits the opportunities that would arise between countries in good standing with one another.

These issues are of concern to all Pacific countries. including those on the rim such as Australia and New Zealand. Because of Fiji's size, geographic centrality in the Pacific, and history, it is a transport and communications hub for the entire Western Pacific. It hosts several organisations that are important to Pacific countries, such as the Pacific Islands Forum Secretariat and various agencies of the United Nations. Other institutions, such as the University of the South Pacific, and businesses, such as Fiji Airways (formerly Air Pacific), serve the wider Pacific but are centrally located in Fiji. A deeper concern is that instability can spread, so that although Pacific countries are insulated from one another by distance and differing concerns, more serious trouble in Fiji could provoke unrest in other places.

What We Would Pray For

Aristotle often uses the phrase, 'what we would pray for', to indicate the goal of people seeking the political arrangement that would give them the best life possible. This does not mean that Aristotle is neglectful of the difficulties of history, culture and geography, but it does imply that people and their leaders should seek an

---

and Governance in Melanesia Program, Studies in State and Society, Number 4 (Canberra: ANU E Press, 2009). The various constitutions are readily available on the internet. The 2013 constitution is at <http://www.fiji.gov.fj/>, accessed 6 August 2013. A commentary on the 2013 *Constitution of the Republic of Fiji* by the Citizens' Constitutional Forum, *An Analysis: 2013 Fiji Government Constitution*, is available at <http://news.ccf.org.fj/>; accessed 6 August 2013.

outcome that will be advantageous in the long term. Otherwise, they will spend generations squabbling over immediate needs and manoeuvring for short-term advantages. Achievement of the goal has both a technical dimension (seen in the constitution and other laws), and a moral dimension (seen in the willingness of people to articulate and strive for the goal).

Given the issues raised above, a suitable goal for the people of the Fiji Islands at the present time would be the formation of a stable and racially harmonious political community or country. Such a community needs to be one, but not homogeneous in the way a family or clan might be. Part of the strength of a political community is that it brings together people who are different and who have different capacities in order that they might contribute to creating a better life for all. The community and its unity are defined by the constitution, and as we will see in Chapter Five, it will be stable if the majority of the people and the different parts of the community all love the constitution.

Love of the constitution is a response to the experience of doing well under the constitution. In other words, when people judge that they have received a fair share of the various goods that are available to the community, they will be content. This includes material goods but also less tangible goods, such as the ability to excel, which flows from education and opportunity. First among the goods is political justice, which implies fairness in participation in the governing of the community and so the opportunity to hold office and have a say in how the community organises itself and plans its future. Other goods will flow from this. The difficulty for all communities and for Fiji in particular is that people in the community differ from one another so that the manner of their participation in the life of the larger community is achieved in various ways. How can this be arranged fairly, keeping in mind both the claims of the parts of the community and the overall happiness of the whole community?

The Problems of Fiji

Today the presenting constitutional problem in Fiji is balance between the indigenous Fijian population and the Indo-Fijian population, but to take this as the sum of the problems is misleading. It is arguable that Fiji has never achieved the unity of a single community. Part of the reason for this is geographical. Fiji consists of an archipelago of more than three hundred islands, of which over one hundred are inhabited. The larger and higher islands of Viti Levu and Vanua Levu are in the west, and in the east the Lau Group stretches south and east towards Tonga. In ancient times, contact between the different islands was possible by canoe, which allowed for war, trade and even alliances, but there is little to suggest that unity was ever achieved, and some islands of the Lau Group had closer relations with Tonga than with western Viti Levu.

These things were evident at the time of cession to the British in 1874. Increased European settlement from 1860 brought calls for more unified government to replace forty or so small chiefdoms. Cakobau, the High Chief of Bau, working with eleven other major chiefs, mostly from the east, formed a confederacy to govern the whole of Fiji. It went through various forms, but was at times at war with the hill peoples of the western highlands, and in the end was able to manage neither the costs of government nor difficulties presented by European settlement. Colonial rule came at the request of the Fijians and with considerable reservation on the part of the British. Of the twelve Fijian chiefs who joined Cakobau to sign the Deed of Cession of Fiji to Great Britain, only one was from the west.[3]

The British Crown ruled Fiji for almost one hundred years, during which time gradual changes in administration leading ultimately to self-government were made. Three policies, however, have important implications for the present difficulties. First, the clause in the Deed of Cession (7, 1) that guaranteed the rights and interests of the High Chief was taken to mean, somewhat romantically, the preservation of Fijian life as it was at the time, especially for commoners. Although the high chiefs participated in colonial institutions and grew in status, most Fijians were

---

3. See RA Derrick, *A History of Fiji* (Suva, Fiji: Government Press, 2001). See also Stephanie Lawson, 'Indigenous Nationalism, "Ethnic Democracy", and the Prospects for a Liberal Constitutional Order in Fiji', *Nationalism and Ethnic Politics* 18/3 (2012): 293–315.

governed indirectly through the Native Fijian Administration and remained living in their villages largely excluded from a developing national economy. At the time of independence, this policy was able to be used by the Fijian leadership to reinforce the claim of Fijian paramountcy, namely, the claim that the indigenous Fijian community should be always dominant in an independent country, although this was not strictly in the original deed. Secondly, although the Deed of Cession (5) allowed for the Crown to take land as needed, early policy established that, with few exceptions, land not already alienated would remain under native title. Thirdly, because it was British policy both that the colony should be able to sustain itself financially and that Fijians would be left to their traditional forms of life, the administration felt compelled to bring some sixty thousand Indians into the colony between 1879 and 1916 to work in the sugar industry. About half chose to remain.[4]

This history has led inevitably to a society in which there are fault lines between different groups of people: between Fijians from different parts of the country; between chiefs and commoners; between Indo-Fijians and indigenous Fijians; between those of different religions or of different subgroups within religions— Christian (Methodist, Catholic), Hindu, Sikh, Moslem; and more lately between those who live in the city and those who live on traditional lands in traditional ways. There are of course other fault lines, and the role of the military forces is extremely significant. While in one sense it is difference that drives the political process as different groups contend for what will be in their own best interests, the good of the whole requires a constitutional accommodation with which all can live. As events since independence in 1970 have shown, this is far from easy and is sure to involve change for each of the groups that is involved.

The Constitutions

As we noted earlier, Fiji has had four constitutions since independence in 1970. The 1970 Constitution grew out of the

---

4. See Ralph R Premdas, 'Seizure of Power, Indigenous Rights and Crafting Democratic Governance in Fiji', *Nationalism and Ethnic Politics* 8/4 (2002): 16–36.

existing colonial arrangements for governing Fiji as well as years of sometimes secret negotiation between Britain and the leaders of both Fijian and Indo-Fijian political parties. As Brij Lal states:

> The final constitution was in its most fundamental aspects an extension of the principles and interests that underpinned the 1966 constitution. It preserved the status quo: paramountcy for Fijians, privilege for Europeans and parity for Indo-Fijians.[5]

The 1990 Constitution followed the military coups of 1987, which had reacted to the election of an Indo-Fijian party to government. The indigenous Fijian establishment could not allow that they be ruled by Indo-Fijians. This is reflected in the Preamble of the Constitution:

> And whereas events in 1987 in Fiji led to the abrogation of the 1970 Constitution. And whereas those events were occasioned by a widespread belief that the 1970 Constitution was inadequate to give protection to the interests of the indigenous Fijians, their values, traditions, customs, way of life and economic well-being.

The 1997 Constitution was the outcome of a review of the 1990 Constitution that was mandated by the constitution itself but which also became politically necessary because of the strong racial tones of the 1990 Constitution. The government set up a Constitutional Commission with broad goals:

> The Commission shall review the Constitution promoting racial harmony and national unity and the economic and social advancement of all communities and bearing in mind internationally recognised principles and standards of individual and groups rights.[6]

---

5. Brij V Lal, *A Time Bomb Lies Buried: Fiji's Road to Independence, 1960–1970* (Canberra: ANU E Press, 2008), 77.
6. Terms of Reference, quoted in Jill Cottrell and Yash Ghai, 'The Role of Constitution-Building Processes in Democratization' (Stockholm: International IDEA, 2004), <http://www.idea.int/conflict/cbp/>, accessed 6 August 2013.

The new constitution was written after extensive consultations that resulted in the Reeves Report and after deliberations by parliament.

The 2013 Constitution was prepared in time for elections in 2014. The 1997 Constitution was suppressed by President Josefa Iloilo in 2009, following the 2006 coup by Commodore Bainimarama. A process was initiated for the writing of a new constitution, which included the National Council for Building a Better Fiji, extensive consultation and the Peoples Charter for Change, Peace and Progress. The Constitution Commission completed a Draft Constitution of Fiji, 2013, but this was rejected by the Bainimarama Government, which put forward its own Draft Constitution of Fiji. The final constitution was established by the government following significant amendments to its own draft and was signed into law by President Epeli Nailatikau in September 2013.

Participation

It would take a long time to make a detailed analysis of the differences between these constitutions. We would have to consider citizenship, the legislature, the method of election, the structure of the executive authority, the judiciary, significant officials, balance of powers, land ownership, individual and group rights and so on. A snapshot, however, can be caught by examining the composition of the executive and the structure and method of election of the legislature.

Under the 1970 Constitution, the Queen of the United Kingdom held executive power in Fiji, which she exercised through a Governor-General. The Governor-General appointed a Prime Minister, who in his own judgement would be best able to command the support of the House of Representatives. Other ministers were appointed by the Governor-General on the advice of the Prime Minister. Under the 1990 Constitution following the 1987 coups and Fiji's departure from the Commonwealth, a President, who was also Commander-in-Chief of the Fiji Military Force, was appointed by the Great Council of Chiefs to hold executive power, which was exercised by him or by Cabinet. The Great Council of Chiefs had functions under the constitution but was neither constituted nor defined by the constitution. The 1997

Constitution gave formal recognition to the Council of Chiefs. It also added a new requirement that Cabinet be formed from such parties, including opposition parties, who had more than ten per cent of the membership of the House. This change, though unusual, was an attempt to bridge those divisions that fell along racial lines. Under the 2013 Constitution, the President is head of state, but acts only on the advice of Cabinet. He is, nevertheless, Commander-in-Chief of the Republic of Fiji Military Forces.[7] The President is elected by parliament, and the Prime Minister is the leader of the political party that has at least fifty per cent of the seats of parliament or the member who receives fifty per cent or more in a vote by parliament. We can turn now to the legislature.

Under the 1970 Constitution legislative power was vested in the parliament, which consisted of two houses, the House of Representatives and the Senate. Members of the House of Representatives were elected by the citizens of Fiji according to both communal and national rolls. There were three separate communal electoral rolls: for Fijians, for Indians and for people of other ethnicities. Membership of the House was set at twenty-two Fijians, twenty-two Indians and eight others. In a complex electoral system, voters voted both according to communal rolls and according to a national roll. A *first-past-the-post system* of counting was used. The Senate contained twenty-two members who were appointed by the Governor-General, eight on his own advice, seven on the advice of the Prime Minister, six on the advice of the Leader of the Opposition and one on the advice of the Council of Rotuma, representing the ethnically distinct Rotumans.

The 1990 Constitution retained the two Houses of Parliament but made the President part of parliament and significantly changed the ethnic balance of the parliament in favour of Fijians. For the House of Representatives, voters on four communal rolls elected thirty-seven Fijians, twenty-seven Indians, a Rotuman and five others. Thirty-four senators were appointed by the President—twenty-four on the advice of the Council of Chiefs, one on the advice of the Rotuma Island Council, and nine on his own judgement from other communities, taking into account their special interests.

---

7. This is a significant change from the Draft Constitution, which had the Prime Minister as Commander-in-Chief of the Fiji Military Forces.

The 1997 Constitution maintained the same structure of the executive but changed the electoral mix. In the House of Representatives, it retained forty-six places for members elected from communal roles—twenty-three Fijians, nineteen Indians, one Rotuman and three others. Twenty-five places were reserved for those elected by all communities on an open electoral roll. It mandated the *alternative vote* or *preferential system of counting*, such as is used in Australia.

The 2013 Constitution reduced parliament to a single House and abolished the communal electoral rolls. It also abolished electorates in favour of a single national electoral roll and a system of *proportional representation*, which would see seats in parliament awarded to members of political parties in proportion to the number of votes nationally that the parties received.[8] It does allow for independent candidates, but neither an independent candidate nor a political party qualifies for a seat unless it receives five per cent of the vote. The initial parliament had fifty members, but this will increase in proportion to the country's population. The constitution makes no mention of the Council of Chiefs.

What are we to make of these changes? Constitutionally, Fiji has had a turbulent four decades as it has wrestled with the problem of how to give all its citizens with their different interests adequate voice in its government. It is clear that, for the most part, the major divide has been seen as that between indigenous Fijian and Indo-Fijian. The 1970 Constitution was constructed to deal with this, seemingly by treating each equally. This did, however, institutionalise politics along racial lines, and when changes in population and in political interests led to the election of a predominantly Indo-Fijian government, the 1987 coups asserted indigenous Fijian dominance. The 1990 Constitution was clearly unbalanced and the 1997 Constitution tried to rectify that but it tried also to bring more governmental co-operation between Indo-Fijians and indigenous Fijians. The 2013 Constitution was far more radical. It abolished communal rolls and made elections more plainly democratic—one vote per person in a national

---

8.   The elimination of electoral districts is a significant change from the Draft Constitution. It makes political parties the principal vehicle for articulating differences in the country. The constitutional arrangements need to be read in conjunction with the *Political Parties Decree 2013*.

electoral roll. Geographical and racial differences were ignored, and the articulation of the interests of different groups was left to the formation of political parties. The government is also stronger. It is not balanced by a Senate, and the President acts only on advice of the Prime Minister. The Council of Chiefs does not have a place in the constitution.

A Technical or a Moral Solution?

As of late 2015, it is not clear whether the 2013 Constitution will ultimately be successful. It does attempt to achieve specific goals, such as stability, racial harmony and the interests of different areas, and its technical finesse shows that the government has received advice of high quality. Its development had been preceded by wide consultation, but in the end it was written by the Attorney General's office and firmly established by the Bainimarama Government without being subject to the people's voice in, for instance, a referendum. Will it be ultimately perceived to be legitimate? This may depend on how well Fijians manage the change and, in particular, on whether they learn to express their differences and seek their interests through new political parties. If it proves to be too challenging to strong interests in the country or too great a change from current arrangements for citizens in general, there may be further constitutional crisis. If that were to happen, it might well be wise for Fiji to institute more flexible constitutional arrangements, such as were attempted in the 1997 Constitution, in order to allow the country to make its way step by step through more gradual constitutional change to a stable future.

It is unlikely, however, that a merely technical solution will work. If a majority of Fiji Islanders and a majority of the various groups in the country are to love the constitution, those persons and groups will need also to come to terms with one another. This is a moral issue, but it is made difficult by the fact that parts of the community can live in isolation from other parts. In a political system, persons and groups seek their own interests, and this gives the process its energy, but they also need to be able to transcend those interests and to look to the good of the whole. If Fiji is eventually to become settled, this challenge needs to be met at all levels of and in all parts of Fijian society.

Chapter Five
The Best Possible and
Best Practicable Constitutions

In Chapter Three, we noted that Aristotle dealt with the question of what is the best constitution by spelling out four meanings of 'the best constitution'—the best possible; the best practicable that most people in most times could achieve; the best that material circumstances might allow; and the best that a particular people might be able to achieve, given their current arrangements. In this chapter we will examine the first two of these. We will also examine his understanding of the kind of justice that we are seeking when we establish political communities. In the next chapter, we will examine the last two senses of 'the best constitution' after first outlining the kinds of conditions and circumstances that affect what can be achieved.

The Best Possible Constitution

Aristotle deals with the best possible constitution in Books VII and VIII of the *Politics*, which present as a fresh study of what the best country or political community would look like. He calls it the country 'one would pray for'. This is the role that it plays in his thought, because although he does not expect that it will be fully achieved often, it stands as a measure and goal towards which all peoples might strive. It is, nevertheless, a real possibility, unlike a Platonic ideal, which cannot be realised. In a sense, it is like the best athlete, a world record sprinter, for instance, whose speed is not often reached, but yet remains a measure for other sprinters. In these books, Aristotle examines the country in terms of his four causes: *material* (people and territory); *efficient* (founders, legislators and education); *final* (the end or good aimed at); and *formal* (the constitution).[1] In this chapter, we will consider just the end and the constitution and leave the material conditions of a country and education to later chapters. We will take up the question of the good again in the last chapter of the book.

The first question we must ask, therefore, is: what is the most choice-worthy way of life? Unless we have a reasonably clear and agreed understanding of this, our efforts to put in place constitutions, laws, policies and practices that will bring about the best life will be confused and haphazard. The question applies both to individual persons and to the country as a whole. Aristotle points out that there are three kinds of good that concern us and among which we can choose: *external goods*, such as wealth, honour and power; *goods of the body*, such as health, strength and pleasure; and *goods of the soul*, such as understanding, courage and prudence, or, in other words, the intellectual and moral virtues. All of these kinds of good are necessary for a full and rich life, but Aristotle notes a strange characteristic of human beings, namely, that they tend to be satisfied with small amounts of virtue (just enough to stay out of trouble), yet to want unlimited quantities of external goods.

What people really want is *happiness*, and the central argument of the *Ethics* is to show that happiness is achieved when human beings attain high levels of virtue, which can be understood as excellence in human functioning. External goods and bodily pleasure are necessary but only in sufficient quantity. Happiness will be achieved when people act justly with one another, are temperate and courageous, and are friendly towards one another. Moreover, the intellectual virtues of wisdom, understanding and prudence enable people to flourish. We might include here the understanding and virtues that flow from religious belief and practice. The country as a whole will also be happier if its people can learn to act in this virtuous way.

---

1. Aristotle develops the theory of four causes in *Physics* II, 3, in *The Complete Works of Aristotle*, edited by Jonathan Barnes. The *material* cause is the matter out of which something is made. The *formal* cause is the 'shape' it takes, though at the level of the thing's essence or nature. The *final* cause is the end or that for the sake of which a thing exists. The *efficient* cause is the maker. Using his example and applying this to a bronze statue, the material cause is the bronze; the formal cause, the shape it is given; the final cause, the profit or enjoyment intended; the efficient cause, the sculptor.

In order to clarify who could rule in this kind of country, Aristotle asks a question about whether the best kind of life is the life of action or the life of thought. In other words, is a better life achieved through involvement in politics, social service, business or the military, or is it had through study, academia and contemplation? Aristotle points out that people given solely to action tend to dominate others and to act as masters focussed on some particular outcome. In politics they tend to become despots and lead their countries into war with their neighbours. People who withdraw into thought tend to initiate little action and will often neglect even their friends and families. The best kind of life, he concludes, is an active life engaged with the affairs of the country, but an active life that is also thoughtful, so that action is based on understanding and on engagement with others through thoughtful conversation.

In determining the constitution of the best possible country, Aristotle first asks what *functions* are necessary for a country to survive. He lists six functions: sustenance (farming and fishing); arts (making tools and structures); arms (military and policing); provision of funds (business); care of the gods (priestcraft); and judgement about action and justice (activities of rulers and judges). These functions define the proper parts of the country. The next issue is about who will be *citizens*. Here Aristotle changes his definition of a *country* from a unit made up of different people to one made up of similar people, and the similarity in the best country is the similarity of those who live lives of intellectual and moral virtue. To do this they need leisure, which excludes farmers, and they need noble activities, which excludes workmen and business people, whose activities Aristotle regards as undignified. Of the three functions remaining, he suggests that the young carry out military and policing functions; the middle-aged, the functions of ruling and judging; the old, the religious functions. The constitution or arrangement of such a country is, therefore, aristocratic, giving voice and political role only to those of liberal education and developed virtue. While many residents are excluded from strict citizenship, if this kind of constitution could be sustained, one could presume that they would be well governed because of the capacity and virtue of the rulers.

An element of aristocratic rule is not unfamiliar in Polynesia, where titles are conferred on the basis of lineages and where those likely to be holders of a title are schooled in the lore, stories and meanings fundamental to the culture. There also exists, at least in some places, a powerful mechanism to ensure that those who assume a title have the necessary virtue or character. In these places, a person may be able to claim a title on the basis of lineage, but has still to be accepted by a vote of other persons, generally those of nobility themselves. There have been cases in which titles have remained vacant, because no such affirmation could be made of the person with the greatest claim to the title. Aristotle would approve of this, because it attaches nobility to character rather than simply to claims on the basis of inheritance.

The Best Practicable Constitution

Aristotle recognises that his best possible constitution would rarely be achieved and that even if it were, it would be unlikely to survive for very long, not least because those who rule could not necessarily ensure that their own children would have the required virtue, but also because in time other elements of the community would compete for rule. He, therefore, has to investigate what we are calling 'the best practicable constitution'. The way he puts the question is instructive:

> What [constitution] is best and what way of life is best for most [countries] and most human beings, judging with a view neither to virtue of the sort that is beyond private persons, nor to education, in respect to those things requiring special advantages provided by nature and an equipment dependent on chance, nor to the [constitution] that one would pray for, but [to] a way of life which it is possible for most to participate in, and a [constitution] in which most [countries] can share?[2]

In other words, what kind of life and what kind of arrangements are most people at most times going to be able to achieve?

Aristotle's answer is that it will be a particular form of *republic*, in which a large middling element is developed in the population. This is sometimes called a middle class, but that term carries connotations

---

2. Aristotle, *Politics* IV, 11 (1295a25–30), 133, substituting 'constitution' for 'regime' and 'countries' for 'cities'.

that Aristotle may not be inferring. We will look first at the form of
the republic in general and then at this more particular form and
Aristotle's arguments for it.

The republic is one of the six pure forms that Aristotle named in
Book III and that we listed in Chapter Four. It is a correct rather than
a deviant form, because rule is for the sake of the people rather than
for the advantage of the rulers. It parallels democracy in so far as
everybody, not just a particular part of the community, participates
actively in the constitution. The name that Aristotle gives it, *politeia*,
often translated or transliterated as 'polity', is the same word that
he uses for 'constitution', which suggests that this form is somehow
normative for a successful *polis* or country. The form, he says, is a
mix of oligarchy and democracy, though it may have some elements
of aristocracy, if virtue is encouraged. His argument is simple. People
claim equality and so the right to have some control over the affairs of
their country on three grounds—freedom, wealth and virtue—which
correspond to the claims of democrats, oligarchs and aristocrats. In
fact, most countries are composed of the poor and the wealthy, so
that the republic, which includes everyone but attempts to achieve a
balance, will largely incorporate these two groups into its constitution.
Aristotle envisages different kinds of republic. Those that tend more
towards oligarchy tend to be called aristocracies; those that tend more
towards democracy tend to be called democracies.

The kind of republic that Aristotle says is the best practicable
is one in which there is a large middling element. Countries are
made up of the very wealthy, the very poor and those somewhere in
between. A republic becomes unstable and moves to extreme forms
when either the very wealthy or the very poor dominate. Drawing on
his definition of virtue in the *Ethics* as a mean between two extremes,
Aristotle shows that the country will be virtuous if it too achieves
a mean, which will occur if the middling group is large.[3] The very
rich tend to rule as masters and not knowing how to be ruled are
inclined to domination; the very poor tend to be ruled as servants
and not knowing how to rule are inclined to fall under the spell of
demagogues, who promise much but care mainly for themselves.
Without a middling group or middle class, the country will be
composed of two groups that are in conflict with one another and

---

3. Aristotle, *Ethics* II, 6, especially 1107a1–3.

neither of whom is able to exercise good political judgement. The likely outcome is tyranny. A balanced and contented country will be formed when most people are at neither of these extremes and so are happy to rule and to be ruled and to relate to one another with some affection. If the middling element is larger than the rich and poor elements, most people will love the constitution, and the country will be free of factional strife and of the likelihood of revolution.

Aristotle's balanced republic blends two otherwise deviant constitutions, namely, oligarchy and democracy, in order to achieve a satisfactory outcome. This is a mark of his realism. Under this constitution, most institutions will include all citizens, for instance, by voting in popular elections, but some offices will be kept for those who are most capable. It is expected, however, that most citizens will feel justly done by, particularly in relation to political voice. We will return to this in Chapter Seven, when we look at political change and how to bring about the best practicable arrangements.

The ideas of this section present a considerable challenge to Pacific countries. Who are the rich? Who are the poor? Who belong to the middling class? One first needs to distinguish two kinds of economy—that based on the basic human need for food and shelter, and that based on money. Let us consider Papua New Guinea as an example. Considered as a money economy, the rich are politicians and those with good jobs in government or business, while the poor are rural people growing their own food. The middling may be those living in the towns on lower wages. Considered as a subsistence economy, the poor are not those living in rural areas but rather those living in settlements around the towns, who are dependent on a money economy and distanced from their gardens but without sufficient money to live well. Depending on how one looks at it, the middling may be either those in rural areas or those on lower wages in the towns, or both. The situation could become unstable if rural people were unable to access basic services in health and education, or if life became too difficult for those living less well in towns, or if too many people had to live poorly in the settlements. This is a significant political problem that will take some years to resolve but which demands attention and care.

Another area of challenge lies in the impact of large foreign owned industrial projects such as those in mining, oil, forestry or fishing.

These projects can be attractive to governments because of the large amounts of tax that they pay, but they can also bring profound changes to people in local areas. On one hand, they may displace people from their traditional lands or make the lands unworkable so that the traditional subsistence economy is no longer viable. On the other hand, they are likely to move people into a different economy as employees in the industry or in subsidiary enterprises. If the industry is sustainable, social and political adjustments can be made, although they will be made well only with serious attention from community leaders and politicians. Many of these industries, however, are either not sustainable or have been conducted in ways that are not sustainable. Mines run out and forests are easily destroyed, if improperly managed. Where will people go, and what means of sustenance will they find, should the industries close down and their lands be no longer productive? These are serious matters that affect the political balance of a country.

Political Justice

The idea of the mixed or blended constitution, namely, a constitution that recognises essentially different parts of a community and apportions opportunity for participation in the life of the community, immediately raises the question of justice. What is the basis for decisions about how to apportion membership of assemblies and appointment of officials? How are the various goods available to the city to be distributed? The question is sharpened because justice itself is a good and, indeed, the highest of the political goods. People like to live justly and are proud when they achieve this in a community. If one listens to political debate, it soon becomes clear that many claims made by people in a community are claims made on the basis of justice.

Justice has to do with the distribution of advantage and disadvantage and is a kind of fairness under which people with equal claim expect to receive equal advantages for equal merit. The difficulty is that different parts of the community make claims on different grounds. The wealthy tend to claim that merit should be determined on the basis of wealth. The multitude of the poor tends to claim that merit should be determined on the basis of freedom or the fact of citizenship, so that all should be equal. The virtuous and well-educated tend to claim that merit should be determined on the basis of capability. The problem with each of these claims, says Aristotle, is that they are partial. Each looks at justice from its own perspective, which contains a presupposition that the difference that distinguishes it from the others is the difference that ought to be the measure of distribution.

Justice in its fullest sense is the happiness of the whole political community. It reaches to individuals, but is also the welfare of the whole community as such—something that Aristotle calls *the common good*. Aristotle reminds us of what a *political community* is:

> A [country] is the [community] of families and villages in a complete and self-sufficient life. This, we assert, is living happily and finely. The political [community] must be regarded, therefore, as being for the sake of noble actions, not for the sake of living together.[4]

Aristotle's expectation is that under a sound constitution this will be achieved, even though different parts of the community make different claims. The political problem is how to bring this about. It can be restated. How can one design a constitution that will ensure participation and justice for all, given that a country is made up of different kinds of persons and that each of them makes some claim to rule?

Aristotle insists that the kind of justice in question is not *transactional* or *commutative*. That is, it is not the kind of justice that flows from a contract and agreement to enter into some form of transaction, such as in business. If it were, the country would be an alliance rather than a community.[5] Instead, what is at stake is *distributive justice*, which pertains to the distribution of the divisible goods of a community and considers the good of all members of the community and of the community as such. This kind of justice does take merit into account, and so the kinds of claims made by

---

4. Aristotle, *Politics* III, 9 (1280b40–1281a3), 99, substituting 'country' for 'city' and 'community' for 'partnership'.
5. Note that this puts Aristotle at odds with theorists of the modern state, who assume some original contract, the social contract, as the source of unity and of claims in respect to justice.

different parts of the community need somehow to be balanced by the legislator. If good law is written, the country will survive shifts of energy and strength in its various parts.[6]

Political justice can be hard to achieve, and where it is not achieved, dissatisfaction can break out into conflict or simmer under the surface. In Guam, which has a population of approximately 160,000, 37 per cent are Chamorro, 26 per cent are Filipino and the remaining 37 per cent are of Pacific Islander, Asian, European or mixed ethnicity. Guam hosts large American air force and naval bases and in 2012 housed 6500 military personnel. At present things are peaceful, though the Chamorros struggle to maintain their identity and many feel set upon. Guam enjoys an American lifestyle, but one can ask whether it might become restless if the economy weakened or if increased numbers of troops caused social disruption.

Returning to Aristotle, the achievement of a balance between the various parts of the community is a matter of practical judgement or prudence, to be exercised by legislators and rulers. It is not something of which philosophy can determine the detail. Nevertheless, Aristotle offers two dialogues that show the ways in which the different parties, in this case, the few and the many, argue about the issues. Each party argues on the basis of the virtue that it has. In the first dialogue, he asks whether the multitude either as a whole or by election should be admitted to the highest deliberative body in the country. One side says no, because these are largely the poor without wealth or great education and their judgement in important things will not be good. The other side argues that the multitude as a whole can exercise better judgement than the few, because, although none of them individually has great skill, as a group the skills and judgement that they have outweigh that of the few better educated or wealthy people. In today's world, this is a good argument for popular elections to parliament.

In the second dialogue, Aristotle asks who should be given particular offices in government. Again he points out that the rich will demand them on the basis of their wealth and contribution to the country in taxes. The poor will demand them on the basis of their citizenship and freedom. The well-born will demand them on the basis of their nobility. Aristotle finds fault with each of these claims and offers an analogy. Should one give the best flute to the most

---

6. For a full discussion of justice in its various kinds, see Aristotle, *Ethics*, Book V.

handsome or tallest person, or should one give it to the best flautist? Similarly, if one is to choose a military commander, one will not look for wealth or citizenship or nobility, though these will not be excluded and some of them may offer advantages, but rather for expertise in soldering and command. The point is clear. The appointment of officials should look to capacity.

We have examined in this chapter Aristotle's best possible and best practicable constitutions and raised the questions of justice that arise once one adopts a mixed constitution or a constitution that takes account of differences between different groups in the community. In the next chapter, we will look at the material conditions of a country and discuss how they limit what is possible for a particular people in a particular place at a particular time.

Chapter Six
The Material Conditions of Political Life

In the last chapter, we investigated both the constitution 'one would pray for' and the best practicable constitution, which is what Aristotle would encourage most peoples to strive for. In this chapter, we will look at the two other senses of the best, namely, the best that circumstances will allow and the best that a particular people may be able to achieve. In order to do this, we will first look at the material conditions that affect what a country can achieve. In a final section, we will look at monarchical forms of rule and the place that they might play in the life of a people.

The Material Conditions of a Country

Aristotle treats the material conditions of a country in Book VII of the *Politics* as part of the discussion of the best possible constitution and of the conditions necessary to live under it. As he says, 'it is impossible for the best [constitution] to arise without equipment to match'.[1] The matter or stuff out of which a country is formed is its human population and the land that it has available to it. The number and character of the people and the size and quality of the land will do much to determine what is possible. Aristotle acts strategically in raising this topic under the heading of the best possible constitution, because it enables him to define his questions and to imagine a benchmark for all countries. He does not give a lot of detail, however, because, as he says at the end of the discussion, it is pointless to give too much detail, because whatever we might pray for, what actually

---

1. Aristotle, *Politics* VII, 4 (1325b37), 203, substituting 'constitution' for 'regime'.

comes about is from the legislator's point of view a matter of chance.[2] In other words, we have to make the best of the land that is given to us.

How many people should a country have? Aristotle argues first against those who presume that the larger a country is the greater it will be. It may be that a larger country can marshal more soldiers than a smaller country, but the key issue is capacity to function in the way that a country should. A country's task is to foster a kind of life in which its citizens will be happy and flourish and to be self-sufficient in doing this. If a country is too small, it will not be able to do this, because it will not have the human capacity to do everything that a country needs to do. On the other hand, if a country is too large it will cease being a political community, because the people will have no way of knowing one another and even the leaders will not be able to select people of talent as officials. Aristotle therefore suggests a benchmark. The best size for a country is reached once it has sufficient people to live well as a political community. Countries can be larger but not indefinitely larger.

Similar considerations apply to the quantity of territory a country might have. It needs to be sufficient for a people who can live as a political community, but it should not be so large that it cannot be surveyed and managed. Again, the minimum requirement is not simply a matter of the area of dry land, but rather that there be sufficient of the kind of land that can supply the needs of the community. A country in Aristotle's definition is a community that can be self-sufficient, and so ideally a country will have areas that allow different kinds of farming and husbandry and that will supply minerals, building materials and similar resources for its main needs. Of course, countries trade with one another for the things they do not have, and so it is advantageous to have an excess of some things that can be traded with other countries. Still, Aristotle's measure is that the people be able to live well but with moderation and that they will have sufficient leisure to engage in cultural pursuits, all of this sustained by what the country itself can produce.

One might wonder what Aristotle would think of enormous modern countries such as the United States of America. The United States has found ways to survive politically, namely, by having a

---

2. Aristotle, *Politics* VII, 12 (1331b18–21), 216.

federal system of government in which certain activities are handled
by the US Government for the whole country but others are allocated
to smaller more local governments, namely those of states, counties
and cities. As well, modern means of communication and transport
have made larger countries than Aristotle could envisage possible.
Still, he would probably have reservations about whether such a
large country could really live as one people. He would also note the
amount of wealth that has been generated and wonder whether such a
people could live moderately. He might also ask how in modern large
democracies, in which mass culture dictates that people do much the
same things, a thoughtful and cultured life might be possible.

Of course, population and size of territory are related, and land is
given, not made. Aristotle makes much of a territory needing well-
defined natural boundaries such as oceans, mountains and large
rivers, so that there are not disputes about boundaries and so that
the territory can be more easily defended. History would seem to
show him to be right, and so some of the political art will be to devise
means of government and styles of life that suit countries of various
sizes. This will include policies that ensure an adequate but not too
great a population. Other issues critical to the territory are its access
to the sea and to means of transport, and the closeness and character
of neighbouring countries. These will impact on both security and
trade.

Aristotle gives attention to how land might be distributed and
where cities and towns might be best placed and configured. There
needs to be a clear balance between land that is in private hands and
land that is owned commonly or publicly. He does not go into detail,
because, as he says, everything has been tried and we can look at what
has been successful. Nevertheless, the distribution needs to be fair
both for persons and families, so that all may survive, and for the
community as a whole, so that its functions can be well performed.
A difficulty with many cities is that they have grown from small
towns and are no longer well sited, because they have outgrown the
space available. Where there is the luxury of planning in advance, a
city should be placed according to the criteria of health, including
especially the availability of water; comfort in the prevailing climatic
conditions; the facilitation of political activities and the possibility
of adequate military defence. He seems to prefer a hillside that gets

the best light and gentle breezes. Internally, spaces and buildings to do with political activity, religion, marketing, industry and transport should be separated and be appropriate to the activities they foster.

In considering the character of the people, Aristotle sets up a dichotomy between spiritedness and thoughtfulness. We can quote his own words:

> The nations in cold locations, particularly in Europe, are filled with spiritedness, but relatively lacking in thought and art; hence they remain freer, but lack political governance and are incapable of ruling their neighbours. Those in Asia, on the other hand, have souls endowed with thought and art, but are lacking in spiritedness; hence they remain ruled and enslaved.[3]

He goes on to claim that the Greek people, particularly the Athenians, stand in between spiritedness and thoughtfulness, and so are both free and well governed. We do not have to accept his conclusion, but the argument highlights the issue of the character of a people and its impact on political possibilities. Character is partly a matter of temperament, but it is also a matter of culture. For our purposes, *culture* can be defined as the learning that a people has achieved with respect to living in a certain way in a certain place and with particular neighbours. It is passed on by instruction and habituation and is deeply entrenched in the practices and meanings of the people. If one considers that grandparents teach grandchildren and those grandchildren teach their grandchildren, culture and custom are very powerful determinants about how a people will act. Political hopes and judgements have to take this into account.

Other Senses of the Best Constitution

The discussion in the last section provides a sense of how Aristotle would deal with 'the best that circumstances will allow'. It is often a matter of geography—the size and disposition of the land, the proximity and character of neighbouring countries, the placement of towns and cities, the availability of farmland, and the presence of

---

3. Aristotle, *Politics* VII, 7 (1327b23–8), 208.

mineral and other resources. These issues need to be reviewed on a country-by-country basis, and often a deficiency in one area will be made up for by strengths in others. Perhaps the easiest way to grasp Aristotle's thought is to note a few examples from the Pacific.

Cook Islanders are justifiably proud that they have been able to sustain a way of life that is successful for small numbers of people living on tiny islands for thousands of years. Cook Islands is composed of a population of approximately twelve thousand people living on fifteen islands with a total of 237 square kilometres of land spread over two million square kilometres of sea. It might have been thought to be unlikely that it could be a vibrant republic in the Aristotelian sense, yet it has found a way to prosper. Cook Islands is a self-governing country in free association with New Zealand. This arrangement with a much larger neighbour enables it to survive in the modern world.

Nauru, by contrast, faces a difficult future. With an area of twenty-one square kilometres and population of just over nine thousand, it was once rich in phosphate, but that resource has run out, and the wealth it created has run down. Nauru is now heavily dependent on aid. Fiji, on the other hand, has a greater land mass, significant resources and a central position in relation to Pacific transport routes. I argued in Excursion Two that Fiji's political problems are in part due to its geography, which sees it composed of large islands in the west, and a string of smaller islands in the east, which are in close proximity to Tonga.

One could well imagine a number of Pacific countries doing well in the Aristotelian sense because their islands are large enough and endowed with sufficient farming land and other resources. They have significant fisheries. Indeed, countries such as Samoa and Tonga and the islands of Vanuatu were clearly able to satisfy their needs before European contact. Being part of the modern world, however, presents other difficulties. None of these countries are likely to be able to generate the massive economies of the Modern European State, but the people do want some of the benefits of technological industrialisation such as medicine, electronics and heavy machinery like cars and boats. This raises the question of how they might generate the income to purchase these kinds of items. We will return to this in Chapter Nine, but the political point is that it makes different kinds of alliances important. The Pacific Forum has pioneered ways in which

Pacific countries can work together, for instance, to purchase and transport oil. Relations with the larger countries of the region, such as Australia and New Zealand, are necessary but sometimes difficult. Foreign aid can be helpful, but it undermines a country's claims of independence and self-sufficiency.

Aristotle's fourth sense of the best, namely, the best that a particular people may be able to achieve, brings to the fore questions of culture and history as well as the question of the constitution under which they presently live. It also engages the question of the actual make-up of the people residing in the territory. If they are to be happy as a whole under a constitution, that constitution will need to take account of the different groups in the community. Aristotle enunciates a principle:

> The part of the country that wants the constitution to continue must be superior to the part not wanting this. Every country is made up of both quality and quantity. By quality I mean freedom, wealth, education and good birth; by quantity, the pre-eminence belonging to the multitude.[4]

The constitution will survive and function effectively only if those who support it are superior to those who are against it. The meaning of 'superior' is deliberately ambiguous. Elsewhere, Aristotle often says that the constitution will survive only if the people love it, that is, that it suits their make-up, supports their interests and appears to them to be founded on justice. Here, the balance has to be found both quantitatively and qualitatively. If, for instance, a people have a form of nobility based on virtue and respect it, one will expect some element of aristocracy in their constitution. The strength entailed in superiority can take many forms but is not usually one of force or the use of arms, which would quickly lead to tyranny.

In the next chapter, we will investigate how constitutions and countries can be changed for the better, but the point of this section is that the legislators need to start with the actual character and make-up of the people and with their existing constitution. In the rush of constitution writing that followed the independence of a number of Pacific countries in the 1960s and 1970s, many countries

---

4.   Aristotle, *Politics* IV, 12 (1296b16–18), 136, substituting 'country' for 'city' and 'constitution' for 'regime'.

found themselves with European-styled constitutions that did not closely reflect the way in which the people had lived and governed themselves. This is particularly obvious in Papua New Guinea, where a large central government sits in Port Moresby without road access to much of the country and tries to cope with enormous complexity of geography, language and culture. In the villages, life goes on in the traditional ways. History and geography may not have offered much alternative to the fragmented nature of the country, but in time there will need to be integration between these different ways of life. Since culture is a strong determinant of how people act, change can only be gradual.

Monarchy

Something that does mark Pacific countries out from others is a tradition of chiefs, and many still function at the village and district level with significant support of the general population. Tonga is ruled by a constitutional monarch and the nobility is powerful, though, in recent years, the King has been under considerable pressure to introduce more democratic reforms. Let us now examine Aristotle's thought on monarchy or the rule of one person.

Monarchy is not Aristotle's first choice of constitution for people who live in a land that has sufficient material resources and who are educated and capable of participating in political life. Nevertheless, he can envisage situations in which monarchy is appropriate. The deviant form of monarchy, *tyranny*, in which one person rules others who remain voiceless solely for his own good, is never far from his mind as a condition that can afflict people if things get out of hand. Yet, he can see that the correct form of monarchy, which he calls *kingship*, can suit some peoples either always or at certain times. In particular, he recognises that small communities, which are not much larger than extended families, may function better under kingship.[5] As well, he sees kingship as a possible developmental stage that might lead on to aristocracy and eventually a republic as people become more capable of rule and especially if population and territory are increased. In an

---

5. Aristotle assumes that political leaders are male, but today political leaders, irrespective of the type of rule, may of course be female or male. As readers of Aristotle, we should keep in mind this difference in circumstances.

extreme case, he recognises that if a person or a family of truly 'god-like' virtue were to emerge, it may well be that it would be just and natural for them to rule as kings.

There are different kinds of kingship and Aristotle describes five, though more could be listed. They range from the Spartan kingship, where in normal times the king has limited powers but in time of war absolute power, to absolute kingship, where the king controls all facets of life. Aristotle separates them on the basis of whether people are willing to be ruled or are ruled by force, whether the kingship is hereditary or elected, and whether the king rules by his own will or according to law and custom.

Kingship is healthy so long as the people are willing to be ruled in this way, but although force might sometimes be needed, the more a king turns to force, the closer the kingship comes to tyranny, which ultimately is unsustainable and unjust. Kingships are more commonly hereditary, although this presents problems, because a family cannot always ensure that its children will be as capable and as virtuous as kingship demands. If kingships become completely elective, the constitution has already moved to another form and the kingship is simply a measure of the powers enjoyed by the king. There is, however, room for a blended manner of appointment in which both inheritance and election or confirmation play a role.

On the question of law, Aristotle asks 'whether it is more advantageous to be ruled by the best man or by the best laws'.[6] If the laws rule, the advantages are that they are the same for everyone and are written carefully and intelligently, away from the pressure of an immediate need for decision. They are, however, universal in scope and may not meet each case well. If a person rules, the risk is that a poor decision will be made with passion in the heat of the moment and that some people may be unjustly favoured. Nevertheless, even with laws in place, many matters will require human deliberation and judgement.

The task of being a king or a queen or a chief is not easy. Aristotle suggests that the difficulty lies in the need for voluntary acceptance of the rule by the people and in the fact that monarchical rule is generally for life. The things that undermine kingship are anger and contempt. If members of the community are harmed or dealt with

---

6. Aristotle, *Politics* III, 15 (1286a8), 111.

unjustly, their anger will move them to rebellion. If the king behaves badly, people will hold him in contempt and soon his authority will weaken. A king, therefore, has to be a person of great virtue and so both hold the respect of the people and himself respect them. If too much force has to be used, the kingship will soon collapse into tyranny and the community will disintegrate or overthrow the tyrant. Aristotle suggests that in order to survive, a king needs to live as a kind of steward of the well-being of his people and also to share his authority with others who are respected in the community.

Aristotle suggests that it is natural for peoples to grow beyond monarchical rule. As a population grows, a king needs the assistance of others in exercising rule and these people need to be educated. If they prove to be virtuous and become engaged with the affairs of the community, the constitution has already shifted towards aristocracy. As more people become educated and capable of participating in the political life of the community, it is likely to move towards being a republic. Aristotle warns that if, on the other hand, wealth is made too important, it may become an oligarchy. The movement from monarchy to more popular forms is natural and just. As Aristotle says:

> It is evident that among similar and equal persons it is neither advantageous nor just for one person to have authority over all matters, regardless of whether there are laws or not and he acts as law himself, whether he and they are good or not, and even whether he is better in respect to virtue—unless it is in a certain manner.[7]

The last phrase of this quotation indicates that Aristotle keeps open the possibility of a person of truly exceptional capacity and virtue arising, which, if it is recognised and accepted by the people, is likely to move the constitution back to something more kingly.

We have now completed our survey of the four senses of the best constitution. In the next chapter we will examine political process and how constitutions change both for better and for worse. Before doing this, however, here are some questions that summarise what

---

7. Aristotle, *Politics* III, 17 (1287b40–1288a5), 115.

we have covered so far and that can assist us in analysing a particular country and constitution.

(1) From what people or peoples is the country composed?

(2) What is the geography of the place, and how does this affect living there?

(3) What is the culture of the people, and what modes of action are important to them? What is their character? If there is more than one culture in the country, how do they relate, and how does this affect the community as a whole?

(4) How does their history affect the ways in which the people live and associate?

(5) What are the essential and incidental parts of the population?

(6) How do they live? What do they hope for?

(7) How does the country's economy work?

(8) What is the existing constitution of the country?

(9) With what other countries does it interact and form alliances, and what effect do these have on its life?

Excursion Three
Tonga: Stability, Chance and Change

This excursion will draw lessons from two outstanding books on the history of Tonga by Ian C Campbell.[1] The first, *Island Kingdom: Tonga Ancient and Modern*, charts Tonga's history from its origins up until the mid-1990s. The second, *Tonga's Way to Democracy*, offers detailed analysis of the political change that began with calls for a more democratic form of government in the 1980s and concluded with the 2010 amendments to the constitution. It is, indeed, fortunate that these histories are available because a grasp of the political development of a country requires a narrative rather than a theory, given that such development depends on who is able to act at a particular time, what they do, and how their actions relate to other events. Some of the connections between events are simply a matter of chance, and their significance may not emerge until later.

The aim of the excursion is not simply to tell the story; we should turn to the history books themselves for that. Rather the aim is to reflect on the history and, in particular, on two moments of that history: the establishment of the 1875 Constitution of Tonga under King Tupou I and the amendments to the Constitution in 2010 under King Tupou V. Although these moments can be fixed with some precision, each of them extends backwards and forwards in time. Why was it that Tupou I was able to unify the kingdom, and to give it a form of government that enabled it alone among Pacific island countries to retain its independence during the period of

---

1. Ian C Campbell, *Island Kingdom: Tonga Ancient and Modern*, 2nd edition (Christchurch: Canterbury University Press, 1992) and *Tonga's Way to Democracy* (Christchurch: Herodotus Press, 2011).

European contact and colonisation? How did it come about under Tupou V that Tonga changed rather suddenly from monarchical and aristocratic government to a more democratic form?

Tongan pre-history is important, because it was then that Tongan culture was first formed, and although cultures change and communities go through periods of both stability and instability, they invariably look back to their origins. Campbell paints a picture of a seafaring people of pioneering culture, who travelled out of Asia nearly three thousand years ago and settled in Tonga, Samoa and Fiji. They brought plants and animals to islands that were too far from the continents to have well-developed flora and fauna. The islands of Tonga consist of two chains of volcanoes related geologically to the junction of the Australian and Pacific Plates. The most populated islands consist of coral limestone that were formed on the tops of submerged volcanoes and then uplifted. They were made fertile by a thick coating of volcanic ash. The Tongan population seems to have remained stable. Subsequent migrations from the west reached only Fiji, and, though the Tongans remained great seafarers, it was the Samoans, or on other accounts the Hawaiians, rather than the Tongans, who migrated to the Eastern Pacific.

Tongan oral traditions date to around AD 1200. Chief among them is the tradition of the Tu'i Tonga, the mythical first King of Tonga and originator of the lineage that ruled Tonga for some centuries. Two other lines of rulers, the Tu'i Ha'atakalaua and the Tu'i Kanokupolu, were established early. Rule could be difficult in the archipelago because of the distance between the main island groups of Tongatapu, Ha'apai and Vava'u. The tiny Niuas are even further away. Difficulties sometimes led to war, but were more normally managed by appointment of governors, who themselves might in turn become powerful. However, as rank passed through both men and women, marriage was often a way of consolidating power. Within a lineage, rank increased with closeness to actual title holders, who had themselves been required to claim the titles and to be confirmed in them. The society that developed in this period was one of distinct social classes—aristocrats (hou'eiki), chiefs (matāpule), commoners (tu'a) and slaves. These things sit deeply in Tongan culture and affect political possibilities.

Tupou I and the Constitution of 1875

On 4 November 1875, King George Tupou I (lived 1797–1893) promulgated the *Constitution of Tonga*.[2] The Constitution is in three parts: Declaration of Rights, Form of Government, and The Land. Part One abolished slavery and made all—commoners and chiefs, Tongans and non-Tongans—subject to the same law, and certain of a range of freedoms and of a fair trial. All Tongans paying tax were eligible to vote. Part Three vested all land in the King, to be distributed to the estates of Nobles, who in turn made allotments to citizens for housing and food production. Land could never be sold. The form of government set out in Part Two was 'constitutional government under the King', in which the King governed in consultation with his Privy Council, which consisted of the Cabinet, the Governors of Ha'apai and Vava'u, and such others as the King might appoint. Ministers of the Cabinet were appointed by the King for as long as he pleased, and included at least a Prime Minister and Ministers for Foreign Affairs, for Lands and for Police. A Legislative Assembly was composed of the Privy Council, the Nobles and Representatives of the People equal to the number of Nobles. (Originally twenty, in 1914 this was limited to nine of each.) The powers of the Assembly were to enact laws, which required acceptance by the King, and to propose budgets, although it had no power to audit the expenditure of ministries. The Constitution also set up a system of courts, which has continued to develop according to need.

Enactment of the Constitution had significant internal and external consequences for Tonga. Internally, it preserved the aristocracy, but limited it to twenty Nobles and relegated all other chiefs to equality with commoners under the law. Succession to the monarchy was defined in law and so was no longer subject to contest on the basis of lineage and title or even simply of strength. As well, this kind of rule established the Tongan archipelago as a single and enduring kingdom or political community. Tonga was

---

2. The Constitution of Tonga is most readily available as *Act of Constitution of Tonga: 1988 Revised Edition* from the Tongan Government website, <crownlaw. gov.to>, accessed 23 May 2014. This revision incorporates the sixteen amendments that had been incorporated since 1875. The revisions are noted in the text.

no longer simply a chieftaincy held together culturally but always subject to fresh claims to rule, even if tensions would still remain and unity would be challenged. Externally, the Constitution and the formal appointment of ministers gave the kingdom the appearance of a modern state, which made it easier for it to deal with foreign powers. Foreign powers generally colonised Pacific islands in order to exploit resources, for strategic reasons, to protect and control their own nationals or to settle communities that had become unstable. In Tonga's case, there were minimal advantages in respect of the first two reasons, and the Constitution appeared to take care of the last two. Tonga concluded treaties with Germany and Britain in 1876 and 1879 and with the United States in 1888.

How did this come about? Tonga was long used to multiple chiefs and to considerable fluidity in the manner of their succession to power. As well, an archipelago spread across eight hundred kilometres of ocean could be expected to be difficult to unite. The story as Campbell tells it is of a stable, well-organised and strong society in the early part of the eighteenth century that descended into civil war during the last two decades of that century and into the first two decades of the next. It may well have been due to dissension within the Tu'i Kanokupolu lineage, which had become dominant. It was complicated by the arrival of European settlers, by the infectious diseases they brought and by the threat of foreign intervention. In the event, Tāufa'ahau, who took the name George Tupou, finally established himself as paramount chief of each of the main island groups and set about unifying Tonga as a whole. His conversion to Christianity brought a new sense of the sacred and a unifying ethic to Tonga. He showed readiness to seek advice from foreigners about how Tonga might govern itself. The result was a series of law codes in 1839, 1850 and 1862, which gradually accustomed Tongans to the rule of law. These culminated in 1875 with the Constitution, which was written with the assistance of the Wesleyan missionary, Shirley Baker.

It is one thing to put a new constitution in place but another thing to hold on to it. A country working under a new constitution needs to be kept stable until that constitution has become part of a way of life for the people. If we accept Aristotle's analysis, the constitutional form not only affects government but also structures communal relationships and customs. Habits have to be formed, and expectations have to be reshaped. A reading of Campbell's history suggests that this indeed happened but that it was a slow process. Despite the advantages to themselves, commoners did not quickly take advantage of the new laws relating to land but rather continued to live in informal relationships with their chiefs. Those of aristocratic rank did not forget their lineage and the possibilities of rule and status that this could have given them. Expatriate traders were restless under the taxation regime and other limitations on their activities and did not believe that Tongans could work with such complicated laws. The Wesleyan missionaries came into conflict among themselves and with the King, particularly over the King's appointment of the former missionary, Shirley Baker, as Prime Minister. The presence of Catholic missionaries invited attention from the French.

In the event, it was fortunate that King George Tupou I lived such a long life, because his standing and good administration through the likes of Baker kept the regime in place. After his death in 1893, he was succeeded by his great-grandson, King George Tupou II, who was a less capable ruler. It was during his reign that the British forced Tonga to be a protectorate and to accept a consul who would advise the King about good practice. Again, Tonga was fortunate, because Britain, already governing Fiji, did not want to take on another colony unless it was necessary to do so, but was able to provide sound advisors on the technicalities of finance and government. In the end, it was probably only in the long and successful reign of Queen Sālote Tupou III (reigned 1918–65) that Tonga could be said to have become constitutionally settled.

Tupou IV, Tupou V and the Constitutional Amendments of 2010

In 2010, the Legislative Assembly passed three Acts amending the *Constitution of Tonga*, which were in due course assented to by King Tāufa'ahau Tupou V.[3] The changes were substantial and

---

3. *Act of Constitution of Tonga (Amendment) Act 2010*, Act 14 of 2010; *Act of Constitution of Tonga (Amendment) (No. 2) Act 2010*, Act No. 20 of 2010; *Act of Constitution of Tonga (Amendment) (No. 3) Act 2010*, Act No. 39 of 2010; available from the Tongan Government website, <crownlaw.gov.to>, accessed 24 May 2014.

wide-ranging. The new role of the King is 'to reign' rather than 'to govern' (*Constitution*, nos. 17 and 41) and the form of government is 'constitutional monarchy' rather than 'constitutional government under the King' (30). The King, therefore, ceased to have executive power and became restrained by the Constitution. He does, however, retain the right to veto legislation and, in consultation with his Privy Council, to appoint judges.

Executive government is now entrusted to the Prime Minister and Cabinet, who are collectively responsible to the Legislative Assembly (51). The Prime Minister is appointed by the King but on the recommendation of the Legislative Assembly, which votes to determine its recommendation after a general election or whenever the position becomes vacant (50A). Other ministers are to be appointed by the King on the advice of the Prime Minister. The Cabinet must number fewer than half the number of members of the Assembly and a maximum of four Cabinet Ministers can be chosen from outside of the Assembly. The Cabinet is responsible to the Legislative Assembly and the ministers must give an annual report about their portfolios to the Assembly and answer all questions put to them by the Assembly (51).

Legislative government remains with the Legislative Assembly, but its composition is significantly changed. It is composed of nine Representatives of Nobles (unchanged from 1914), of seventeen Representatives of the People (up from nine) and of all of the Cabinet (59 and 60). Members of the Privy Council are no longer members of the Legislative Assembly. Elections are required at least every four years (77), and *every* Tongan living in Tonga of twenty-one or more years of age is eligible to register and to vote (64): requirements to do with land leases and literacy are no longer in place.

These changes are momentous and constitute a revolution in the Aristotelian sense, though not like the violent and disruptive revolutions of the eighteenth and nineteenth centuries in Europe, which ushered in the modern form of democracy. The Tongan revolution managed both deep change and consistency with prior practice and custom. It is highly significant that the change proceeded by amendment so that the constitution was amended rather than replaced. The new constitution is truly democratic in the manner of election of the Legislative Assembly and of the government, and the government is accountable to the electorate through the Assembly. The Representatives of the People now have a real voice. They cannot be simply outnumbered and ignored by the Cabinet and Privy Council, which had happened frequently in recent decades. They are no longer limited to being agitators against the government but rather have the opportunity and responsibility to construct Tonga's future. Yet, there are checks on how the legislature might act, as the King can veto legislation, which particularly in such a small country could prevent rash legislative action. Similarly, the requirement that the Speaker be elected from among the Representatives of the Nobles can be seen as a measure consonant with Tongan custom to give the Assembly dignity in its proceedings (61).

How did Tonga come to change in this way? A philosophical reading of Campbell's histories suggests that much credit should be given to King Tāufa'ahau Tupou IV. He, like his father before him, had been Prime Minister to his mother Queen Sālote and had provided the efficient and effective government that had, along with the Queen's own charm and her skill in binding families through marriage, stabilised her reign. When he became King in 1965, Tupou IV continued a program that ensured a high quality of education for Tongans and significant economic development. These in themselves were sufficient to generate the need for change. As we have seen in our Aristotelian analysis, monarchy can be a very satisfactory political form for a small community or for one that is simple in its needs or in an early stage of political development. However, once people are well educated they have reason to expect to be able to participate in decisions about their own futures. Further, when economic activities become complex, government needs to be responsive to economic demands. It is perhaps unfortunate that Tupou IV, whose reign was so long (1965–2006), was not able in his later years to respond to calls for political changes indicated by his social and economic reforms. During a demonstration for democracy in 2005, I experienced the tension in educated people in Tonga between their feelings of deep respect for the King and their sense of urgency for political change that would make the government more responsive and accountable.

Change in Tonga came also through the demands of educated Tongans and a pro-democracy movement, which had its roots in 1986 in responses to government excesses, although there had been tensions from the mid-1970s. The immediate triggers were the award by the government of exceedingly high overtime payments to members of the Legislative Assembly who travelled to their constituencies to explain a new tax and the sale by the government of Tongan visas to overseas persons. The matters were challenged in the Assembly, but the government, with its numbers, simply ignored the challenges. The movement for reform, therefore, began not so much with a demand for structural reform but with a desire for government accountability. Also in 1986, Tonga experienced its first public demonstration, which though moderate in its agenda showed public concern about the government's conduct. Demonstrations and petitions were to be a feature of Tongan politics for the next twenty years, and although largely ignored by king and government, they gradually led to consensus among the people and eventually exerted such pressure on the government that change was inevitable.

A key figure in this movement was 'Akilisi Pohiva, who, in 1986, had recently returned from the University of the South Pacific, in Fiji, where he had been exposed to new political ideas. A controversial figure, he was often in and out of court suing or being sued for libel, being prosecuted by the government or challenging a government action. Although never able to form a stable group of collaborators, he remained central to the fight for democracy until 2010 and throughout his political career he consistently polled well in elections. After the 2010 election he was appointed to cabinet but resigned in protest in 2011. In 2014, he became Prime Minister.

Such significant political change requires a marked degree of consensus among the whole population despite their diverse interests and different opinions. Compromises have to be made and agreement reached. The final change has to be carefully drafted into law to ensure that there are no unintended consequences to the changes introduced by the new law. This requires an extended process, which takes time. A National Committee for Political Reform (NCPR) had canvassed the opinions of Tongans in Tonga and overseas. Its report was delivered to King Tupou IV on 2 August 2006, just before his death, and to the Legislative Assembly on 2 October. The new King, Tupou V, announced within days of his father's death that he would give up most of his executive powers. The government announced a Tripartite Committee of members of government, Nobles and People's Representatives to work on the report of the NCPR and to reach a consensus. At the same time, the government released its own response to the report and a proposal for change, as did Pohiva. Release of these proposals was probably a mistake, as they seemed to interfere with the task of the Tripartite Committee. It may have been partly responsible for the tragic riot and burning in the main town, Nuku'alofa, on 16 November 2006. Ultimately, the Tripartite Committee did its work and a Constitutional and Electoral Commission of experts in law was formed to work out the final details of the constitutional changes and to draft the law.

Conclusion

Tonga now has its new constitution, and there is good reason to hope that it will serve the country well. The government and the Legislative Assembly may stumble at first as they learn how to work effectively in accord with new rules. The people of Tonga may be disappointed that life does not quickly change substantially for the better, but they do have a greater say in how decisions affecting them are made, and the government is more accountable. Most importantly, the constitution is Tongan, negotiated in Tonga by Tongans with their understanding of their people and of the land in which they live. Aristotle in his *Politics* refused to work out all the details of a constitution. 'Speaking about them', he said, 'is a work of prayer; having them come about, a work of chance.'[4] Tonga has, in many ways, been fortunate. King George Tupou I in his long reign managed to stabilise and consolidate the country and to hold it together despite restlessness among the chiefs and external pressures. Queen Sālote Tupou III, though not initially expected to be successful as a youthful queen, managed in her long reign

---

4.   Aristotle, *Politics* VII, 12 (1331b18–20), 216.

to bind and settle the country. King Tāufa'ahau Tupou IV brought twentieth-century reform in education and business but was unfortunately in his long reign unable to accommodate political change. King George Tupou V, though unpopular as Crown Prince, in a very short reign allowed political reform to happen quickly.

Chapter Seven
Preserving Constitutions and Countries

In Books V and VI of the *Politics*, Aristotle begins again and this time concentrates not on the formal lines of political thinking with their essential distinctions and workable principles, but on the complexity and dynamics of actual political communities. We have previously seen two apparently contradictory definitions of a country. In Book III, Aristotle defines a country as 'a multitude of persons that is adequate with a view to a self-sufficient life'.[1] The multitude is not simply a matter of quantity; rather, there are qualitative differences between the citizens, and the city is a composite of these different kinds of people. In Book VII, on the other hand, Aristotle defines a country as 'a [community] of similar persons for the sake of a life that is the best possible'.[2] Here in the analysis of the best possible constitution, emphasis is given to the identity between those who share in community because of the excellence of their virtue and the unity of their goals.

In this chapter, we will concentrate on the first definition, which recognises the differences among the many people constituting the country. It is important to grasp what these differences are, the ways in which they are required by the nature of persons and by the needs of the country, and the ways in which these differences might be taken account of when the political structure of the country is formed, so that all persons may be recognised in appropriate ways. We should keep in mind Aristotle's best practicable constitution, the mixed constitution that blends democracy and oligarchy with a touch

1. Aristotle, *Politics* III, 1 (1275b19), 87; see also III, 1 (1274b40), 86, substituting 'community' for 'regime'.
2. Aristotle, *Politics* VII, 8 (1328a35), 209.

of aristocracy but with a large middling class. While many countries do not achieve this, it is an ideal towards which Aristotle would guide them.

Also in this chapter, following Aristotle's Books V and VI, we take account of the fact that constitutions are never static. Countries are composed of people of varying interests and groupings, and their political representatives are of varying capacity. The political question amounts to how these different groups are recognised in the formal structures of the political communities or in participation in assemblies, in voting and in the roles of and access to officials. Seen in this way, a country begins to look like a living organism that moves in many different ways, but which will be healthy when it is so organised that its parts move in concert.

This view is contrary to the claim under the Idea of the Modern State, which posits constitutions that are completely stable. In this view, the movement of the masses is somehow contained by the abstract state, which is immoveable. Echoes of this idea are seen in a country such as Australia, for instance, which is very reluctant to change its formal written constitution, even when there are clear inadequacies in it. But despite this view, there is in fact constant change of laws and of governmental organisation in response to changing circumstances and to changes in government. The original constitution of Papua New Guinea, in contrast, recognised that it is a developing constitution of a country that is itself developing, and so it makes change of the formal constitution easy to achieve.

This chapter will have three parts. The first will examine the different parts of the community, which give rise to different kinds of constitution and to the tensions that drive political activity. The second will look at the process of political change, which is in Aristotelian terms a concern with how constitutions decay and are preserved and at how a stable balance can be achieved. The third will take note of the art of speech-making, which is a singularly most important political tool, and at its role in persuading whole communities to adopt a single course of action.

Variety in Country and Constitution

Whereas in the modern world people often seem to think that there is only one kind of legitimate constitution, namely, democracy, and that all democracies are the same, Aristotle, as we have seen, was aware that countries are formed with much more variation, because of differences in the people, in the land and the opportunities it offers, and in the ways in which a country is formed. It is the differences among people that drive politics, because, as we saw in Chapter Five, everyone seeks justice, but their understandings of justice are not identical. Everyone agrees that justice implies some sort of equality, but equality of what?

The multitude or the people, namely, those who are poor or less well off, identify equality with freedom or citizenship and then assume that because all the people are free they are also equal, so that they have the same claims to participation in the political process and wealth. Those that are well off in terms of property measure equality in terms of wealth and so expect that they will receive more of other kinds of goods, such as participation in politics and honours. For Aristotle, those who are truly virtuous have the greatest claim, but he notes that they do not usually insist on their interests being met, because they are so few and because their virtue makes them less inclined to contest their claims. Finally, Aristotle recognises those who are well born on the basis of the virtue and wealth of their ancestors and who often claim pre-eminence on the basis of their nobility. The far greater numbers of people comprising the multitude and wealthy compared to the numbers of virtuous and noble people usually make democracy and oligarchy the competing forms of constitution.

Political communities, whether democratic or oligarchic or a mixture of both, will vary with the kinds of lives lived by the people in them. Aristotle discusses the differences between communities that are largely given to farming, those given to raising livestock, those given to business and commerce and those largely given to trades and labour, or what we would call industry. Differences of constitution of the community around these poles will build different sorts of communities and the politics will change. Aristotle, himself, prefers the farming communities, because in these the people are occupied with their daily work, which is satisfying and provides their main needs, and enter into political matters less frequently but more carefully. A community of merchants and sailors, however, congregates in the city and has time to get up to political mischief. Where the democratic expectation of 'doing what you want' exists, they are likely to get up to other mischief as well.

Other differences also exist. Aristotle often mentions 'the tribes', people related by family, who identify together and look to common interests. We have seen how, in Books IV and VII, he recognises different functions and persons who carry out those functions that are necessary in the country—food production, trades, military and police, business, religion, courts and parliaments, government officials, merchants and labourers. We could prepare a similar list for our own country, but the point is that the people involved in each of these works will be formed in different ways and will have different outlooks and interests. They are, nevertheless, all part of the one political community, which needs, therefore, to be finely tuned in order to take account of the concerns, action and interests of each of them.

We have already noted the difference in Pacific countries between those who live on traditional lands by subsistence farming and those who live in the towns on salaried employment, often in government positions, or in business. The people have often had very different educational experiences and effectively live in different economies. The differences are not as clear cut as they are sometimes painted in discussions of the 'political elites' and the 'rural poor'. Often well-educated people choose village life for significant parts of their lives, and many of those living in towns are not well off. Nevertheless, there is significant difference and therefore difference of outlook and interest between those who live in rural areas on subsistent economies and those who are well educated and live in towns on money-based economies.

What is at stake for these different people and groups is access to political voice or power and access to services. Access to political voice comes through membership of and voting for important assemblies and through appointment of officials. At the most democratic end of the range of possibilities, everyone would meet to make important decisions and official positions would be distributed by lot in such a way that each person could hold office once only and for a defined period. At the most oligarchic end, power would be held by just a few on the basis of the amount of property they own. Interestingly, Aristotle sees each of these extreme forms as unstable and likely to lead to tyranny. However, often enough people will put up with deviant regimes so long as they receive the things they need to live—food, shelter, health services and education. Nevertheless, the challenge that Aristotle puts is to build a country in which everyone feels that they have both a just level of participation and the services that they need to live. We have already examined his proposal of the best practicable constitution, which is a mixed or blended constitution with a sizeable middle element.

Change and Preservation

Collapses of regime and of constitution often begin with the formation of *factions*, that is, groups of people who identify with one another in a grievance. Conflict then arises between the different factions, and this leads to factional strife. A simple change occurs when one group supplants another in government under the same constitution. Full revolution occurs when factional strife leads to a fundamental change of constitution—for instance, from democracy to oligarchy or vice versa. The fundamental causes of this instability usually have to do with justice and in particular with conflict based on the partial senses of justice that people hold. As we have already seen, the different parts of a community tend to measure justice in a partial kind of way related to their own conditions and interests, and so each party to a dispute will tend to give different answers to the questions facing them. The immediate causes of disputes, however, are often smaller things. Aristotle mentions a few: arrogance or profiteering by those in office; accretion of too much power by one person; fear of punishment or neglect; experience of contempt from other persons or groups; ethnic differences when there is movement of peoples; misbehaviour by political leaders; rivalry between leaders.

There is a sense in which the modern *political party*, unknown to Aristotle, takes over and institutionalises the loose factions of which he was aware. Parties give themselves identity and legitimacy on the basis of a set of ideas, often called an *ideology*. It has been, however, common in the West for parties to be roughly aligned either with the poor or workers, on the one hand, or the rich or employers and owners, on the other. Regular elections are something of a safety valve, so that when dissatisfaction arises in a significant portion of the population, a peaceful change of regime is able to happen through a change of ruling party. Usually new governments change the structure of departments and appoint new judges and heads of statutory bodies of their own choosing so that the change of government does amount to a minor revolution in Aristotelian terms.

As Aristotle sees it, the task of the politician is to preserve the constitution and to think practically about the good life. We might say that it is larger than this in the sense that what it entails is preserving the political community or country and seeing that the people of the country are treated justly, that they live in harmony with one another and that they can live well. One of Aristotle's insights is that this is not an entirely static matter, but rather involves adjustment, although the change involved should be subtle rather than gross. The dynamics of justice, changes in the population, the success or failure of ventures and changes of circumstances of a country call for adaptation when problems arise. Officials make many of the day-to-day decisions of government, but the role of the politician is to monitor outcomes, to see to appropriate appointments and to change structures and policies as the need becomes apparent. Judgements should be made in terms of what is best, and it is here that Aristotle's four senses of the best constitution are again relevant. Catastrophes happen and mistakes are made, but if political decisions lean in some way towards the best practicable or balanced constitution, there can be hope that justice will be achieved in the broadest possible way. If the people then feel that they do well under the constitution, they will love it, and Aristotle says a number of times that this is its best protection. The starting point, however, is the constitution that one has now.

Much of what we have seen in Aristotle is captured in the following definition of *politics* given by Michael Oakeshott:

> Politics is the activity of attending to the general arrangements of a collection of people who, in respect of their common recognition of a manner of attending to its arrangements, compose a single community. To suppose a collection of people without recognised traditions of behaviour, or one which enjoyed arrangements which intimated no direction for change and needed no attention, is to suppose a people

incapable of politics. This activity, then, springs neither from instant desires, nor from general principles, but from the existing traditions of behaviour themselves. And the form it takes, because it can take no other, is the amendment of existing arrangements by exploring and pursuing what is intimated in them. The arrangements then constitute a society capable of political activity, whether they are customs or institutions or laws or diplomatic decisions, are at once coherent and incoherent; they compose a pattern and at the same time they intimate a sympathy for what does not fully appear. Political activity is the exploration of that sympathy; and consequently, relevant political reasoning will be the convincing exposure of a sympathy, present but not yet followed up, and the convincing demonstration that now is the appropriate moment for recognizing it.[3]

At the heart of this description is the notion that the core of political activity lies in amending the existing *arrangements* of a community. The arrangements are all those things that regulate and order how people act together and in relationship with one another. They include laws, legal agreements and written constitutions, but also customs and culture that are held and understood by a people, even if they are not written down. In the broad sense of the term, these are what Aristotle means by the constitution of a political community. The need for change arises because all of these arrangements can never be fully consistent with one another. Normally, we live comfortably with the inconsistencies, but they can become troubling when circumstances change or when an event triggers some kind of crisis.

Oakeshott rejects 'instant desires' and 'general principles' as starting points for change. In doing this, he exposes two opposed positions. The first is that we can do whatever we like, especially if we are excited by a dream for a better world. It takes forms that are either *revolutionary* or *progressive* or both. The second is that we can solve our problems simply by reasoning from general principles, something that is called *rationalism*. Both these positions are presuppositions that afflict the modern world. The rationalist position assumes that it is possible to design a full set of constitutions, laws and customs

---

3. Michael Oakeshott, 'Political Education', in *Rationalism in Politics and Other Essays* (Indianapolis: Liberty Press, 1991), 56-7.

for a 'new' country from scratch and on the basis of political science. The progressive position assumes that sudden new directions can be taken without reference to whatever has already been in place. Both assumptions lead to failure.

Political communities are formed from pre-existing communities, even if they are pre-political communities such as families. The political process necessarily begins from the existing practices of actual people. Effective change will be guided by leaders who have great sensitivity to their people, to their ways of doing things and to the problems that they face. These are people who are able to judge what it is best to do in a particular situation. The arguments they use when proposing change should begin with existing traditions and demonstrate how a proposed arrangement will flow appropriately from these traditions so as to resolve difficulties or to improve the manner in which the community functions.

The Political Art—Speech-Making

What kind of activity, then, is politics? Aristotle distinguishes the active life and the contemplative life. The *contemplative life* is the life of thought, of science and philosophy; we might also include religious contemplation. The *active life* is the life of engagement in the world and in human affairs. Here, Aristotle distinguishes three kinds of activity: *labour* is the involvement with the perishable necessities of life such as food production, which is never-ending; *work* generates artefacts such as buildings or monuments, which endure and are known as the product of their maker, or concrete outcomes such as health, when a doctor treats a patient; *action* generates no product but is rather activity in the realm of human knowledge and relationship. Action does, however, bring change, because, as attitudes and relationships between people change, new human possibilities emerge. This is the nature of the activity of the politician.[4]

Clearly a politician is involved in making judgements and decisions, and so part of the character of a politician is to be prudent, that is to act with good practical judgement that takes account both of matters of principle and of the particular circumstances of the

---

4. See Hannah Arendt, *The Human Condition*, 2nd edition (Chicago: Chicago University Press, 1998). The book is built around this distinction.

moment. But unlike the contemplative, the politician does this in public under the pressure of events, in the midst of a sea of people, each of whom has an interest in the outcomes of deliberation. The art of the politician, therefore, is the art of persuasion, and this takes place through speech-making. The study of this is called *rhetoric*. Although controversy arises around rhetoric, so important did Aristotle believe it to be he wrote a separate book called *The Art of Rhetoric* or simply the *Rhetoric*.

There is good reason to study the speech-making or oratorical arts of various Pacific peoples, because, as one soon learns at a meeting or conference, people from different Pacific countries present differently when they speak in public. Polynesians behave quite differently from Melanesians, and Micronesians speak differently from both Polynesians and Melanesians. On a smaller scale, although they are in many ways close historically and culturally, Samoans speak differently from Tongans. These differences have two kinds of implication. First, one needs to know how to speak persuasively within a culture. Secondly, one needs to know how to speak effectively from within one's culture but to a wider world. We will leave these questions for more detailed study at another time and simply draw some of the more general principles from Aristotle's work.

Aristotle wrote the *Rhetoric* well aware of the disrepute that often followed rhetoricians, who taught their students how to win arguments, often by unfair means, such as by playing to emotions or by making statements that caught people's imaginations but in fact misled them. Aristotle's solution to this was to suggest that rhetoric is not a science in its own right but that it is an art that is ancillary to other arts and sciences and even to good judgement itself. The politician does not, therefore, simply learn how to make speeches, but rather learns various arts and sciences so as to be able to make good judgements and then learns how to present these judgements most persuasively to other citizens. This comes out in Aristotle's definition of *rhetoric* as 'the power to observe the persuasiveness of which any particular matter admits'.[5]

Aristotle distinguishes three kinds of rhetoric. *Deliberative speech* urges the hearer to do something in the future on the basis of its

---

5.   Aristotle, *The Art of Rhetoric*, translated by HC Lawson-Tancred (London: Penguin, 2004), I, 2 (1355b20), 74.

good. Its proper place is in public assemblies and legislatures. It encourages people to choose certain courses of action or to establish certain laws. *Forensic speech* attacks or defends past actions on the basis of justice or injustice. Its proper place is in the courts. It argues that a certain person was guilty or innocent of having performed a certain action that is subject to legal prohibition. *Laudatory speech* praises or censures persons on the basis of honour or dishonour. Its proper place is in public gatherings that recognise people and build communities. It holds up certain persons or actions as worthy of honour or contempt. While any speech may contain elements of each of these genres, the division is based on the purpose of the speech, and so speakers need to be clear about what they are doing and about the outcome they wish to achieve.

Aristotle also distinguishes three ways or means of persuading audiences, and he gives significant weight to each. The first is the *character* of the speaker. We are inclined to believe someone who presents as knowledgeable, virtuous (honest) and friendly to us, because we have sometimes been misled by people with the opposite characteristics. The second is the frame of mind into which the audience is brought, often by stirring *emotions* or raising *interests*. People act on their emotions, and so the speaker needs to influence their feelings. The third is the *logical arguments* that can be made for the case. This gives integrity to the speech, because if the case that is being put has merit, there will be reasons for it, and it is right that people should know these reasons.

Aristotle does, however, recognise the difficulties involved in the process of developing good political argument. Politics is directed at action, and action is directed at the best possible outcome or the good. Knowing what the achievable good might be is not easy, and more often than not science will not provide the answer. This may be because the science is not available (for any number of reasons) or because the judgement to be made is such that science would not help. This is the sense in which we say that politics runs on *opinion*. What we hope for in political leaders is persons who are able to form sound opinions and who are able to persuade others about the validity of these opinions.

Yet the world of politics is awash in opinions of greatly varying quality. We might talk of common opinion and expert opinion, but we have also to acknowledge a multitude of opinions linked to people's interests and prejudices. Some opinions, when held up to the light, are hollow or empty, yet they can, nevertheless, circulate through communities. Part of the political art is to deal with all of these opinions, to weigh them, to sift them for value, to modify them, all in the expectation of coming up with sound opinion and then of being able to persuade others about the best course of action. Rhetorical argument, therefore, is less rigorous and more dialectical than logical or scientific argument, and Aristotle gives considerable attention to the kinds of arguments that will work.[6] Often they are based on past experience or on the kinds of things that tend to happen, once certain other things are done. There are elements of probability involved.

People get into politics for a variety of reasons. Some may enjoy the contest. Others may be passionate about certain issues. Still others may enjoy the level of contact with many people and the honour it brings them. These are secondary and often distracting motives, and so one would hope that most have a broad conception that they can do some good for their country. At root, however, what is needed are politicians who understand the various parts of their political community, who appreciate the good of the country and worth of the constitution and are able to protect and improve it, who are of sound judgement about the kinds of issues the country faces and who are able to persuade people about the best way to proceed. These are people rich in the virtue of *prudence*. As citizens we need to be people who can periodically vote carefully to put people such as these into office.

---

6. See Aristotle, *Rhetoric*, I, 3–8.

Chapter Eight
Nurturing Political Life—Education

The political community exists not for the sake of living as such but for the sake of living well. Living, like any activity, says Aristotle, entails two things—understanding the end or goal and knowing the way to achieve it. If the community and its members are to live well they will need both to understand what living well is and to know how to do the things that will bring about this kind of life. For Aristotle, the goal is *happiness* both of the country as a whole and of each of its citizens. 'Happiness', he tells us, 'is the actualisation and complete practice of virtue, and this not on the basis of a presupposition but unqualifiedly.'[1] Virtue is excellence of intellect and of character. Elsewhere, he criticises those who adopt a 'presupposition', by which he means a partial and concrete view of happiness. The Spartans, for instance, promoted a life and a country that was warlike and were very successful in training their young men for war. They lived well so long as they were at war, but 'came to ruin when they were ruling an empire through not knowing how to be at leisure'.[2]

How do human beings become good and excellent? Aristotle suggests three ways—by nature, habit and reason. *Nature* is important, and Aristotle gives attention to the age at which people should marry in order to have healthy children and to be able to bring them up successfully, how many children they should have, how the children should be fed and what level of exercise will make small children strong. While these are largely matters for medical and other sciences, custom and law ought also to direct people towards

---

1. Aristotle, *Politics* VII, 13 (1332a10), 217.
2. Aristotle, *Politics* II, 9 (1271b5), 78.

the best outcomes. However, human beings do not live just by nature, as would, for instance, simple animals. Rather, in common with some of the higher animals they can form *habits*, which moderate their desires and passions and lead to consistent modes of action. They can also direct their actions by *reason* in so far as by understanding ends and means they can choose how to act. Yet, they are born helpless and must in a few years learn how to act in complex and sophisticated ways. This is a matter of *education*, which consists of the formation of habits or habituation and instruction in the use of reason. Education is a public responsibility because it is for the good of the whole community and teaches people how to live in and for the community.

For educational purposes, Aristotle divides life into four periods—birth to age seven; seven to puberty; puberty to twenty-one; the years of adulthood. Habituation begins soon after birth and continues throughout life. Instruction begins at age seven as children gain the use of reason but is conducted differently before and after puberty. Formal instruction might end at age twenty-one as people enter into adulthood, but learning goes on through practice and reaches its fulfilment in mature middle age through public action and engagement in the arts.

Moral Upbringing—Habituation

At the beginning of the *Ethics,* Aristotle comes to the issue of habit formation via the question, what constitutes a happy life? It is generally agreed, he finds, that happiness is the ultimate good that all human beings seek, but what does that mean? It sounds like a platitude. He canvasses a range of views according to what people say and what they do. People seek things such as wealth, pleasure, health, honour, or power, and different people propose one or other of these to be the ultimate good. But are any of them really ultimate goods rather than subsidiary goods that, when found in moderation, contribute to the ultimate good? Which of them might even be considered goods in themselves rather than simply means? People hoard money, for instance, but the peculiarity of money is that it does us no good unless we give it away in exchange for something else.

Faced with this dilemma, Aristotle begins again. What is a good flautist? It is surely someone who plays the flute well, or, in other words, performs the function of playing the flute well. Similarly, he suggests that if we can discern the functions of a human being, this will lead us to the good, because it will consist in excellence in the performance of human functioning. He adds three qualifications. First, happiness will be found in *activity*, not in a state of mind, because it is activity that achieves good and fulfils function. Secondly, whatever this excellence is, it will not be complete without some *external goods*, such as sufficient wealth, or goods of the body, such as health or beauty. Thirdly, it will be hard to call a life happy unless it is in some sense *complete*. A young person may be content with life at the moment, but happiness properly speaking cannot really be claimed until a life is fully developed and settled. This allows him to define a happy person in the following way:

> One who is active in accordance with complete virtue, and who is adequately furnished with external goods, and that not for some unspecified period but throughout a complete life.[3]

In order to bring more exactness to our understanding of human functioning, Aristotle distinguishes three generic kinds of functioning: *vegetative functions* such as nutrition and growth; *appetitive functions* such as desire for the pleasant and fear of the dangerous and the painful; *intellectual functions* such as reasoning and understanding. The first are not amenable to reason, while the second are not rational in themselves but respond to reason as when, for instance, someone might calm our fear by words or someone might curb our desire for food with an admonition. This allows Aristotle to distinguish between the *moral virtues*, which have to do with actions related to appetite and emotion, and the *intellectual virtues*, which have to do with the exercise of reason. It is with the nature and development of moral virtues that we are concerned in this section.

In order to define *virtue* more closely, Aristotle takes account of four considerations. First, the virtue is not the feeling itself, nor is it the faculty or power that enables us to have that feeling. These two, the feeling itself and the very ability to have such feelings, are simply part of our natural endowment and we are not praised or blamed for having them. Rather it is a disposition or tendency to have the feeling

---

3. Aristotle, *Ethics* I, 10 (1101a15–16), 24.

in a certain way or to a certain degree of intensity. The way we can have the feeling can be praised or blamed, to the extent that it is the outcome of our appropriation of those sentiments. Secondly, the right way to experience a feeling or desire is usually somewhere between two extremes that will be different for different people. Aristotle calls it a *mean* or an average. For example, a virtuous athlete will necessarily and rightly desire and consume more food than someone who does only light work, but what is right for him will still be in between too little and too much. Thirdly, we cannot simply compute where this mean might lie, and so the best guide is how a virtuous person actually reacts to different situations. Fourthly, although they are not brought about simply by reason, virtuous acts are in accord with reason. This allows Aristotle to define virtue in the following way:

> So virtue is a purposive disposition, lying in a mean that is relative to us and determined by a rational principle, and by that which a prudent man would use to determine it.[4]

How then do we attain these virtues? Aristotle insists that virtues are instilled in us by repeated actions. In order to become courageous we need to act in the way a courageous person would even if we are not yet actually courageous and may, in fact, be quite fearful as we do the apparently courageous thing. We may do it simply by imitating someone near us, or we may do it because the law or a superior tells us to do it, or we may do it to achieve the pleasure of a reward or to avoid the pain of a punishment. In time and as we reflect on our experience, such actions become our own. We begin to see that we should act this way and that it is the honourable, decent, and admirable way to be. We now know what we are doing, we choose to do it and how we act is in accord with a firm disposition to act in that way. This is virtue and Aristotle explains that once we have achieved the virtues, we will act justly or temperately or prudently or courageously in a somewhat easy way, almost by second nature, and we will find the action pleasurable, even if acting this way may involve external hardships and painful elements.

---

4.   Aristotle, *Ethics* II, 6 (1107a1–3), 42.

This gives us insight into moral training or the upbringing of children. In the first instance, children tend readily to imitate their elders, and parents and teachers also guide how they act by telling them what to do and by rewards and punishments. Gradually these ways of acting become easy and habitual. Eventually, the child understands what it is doing and acts consistently by choice and so becomes an agent rather than an imitator and can be said to be virtuous. Such habituation begins at an early age. Small babies are gradually taught to sleep through the night without being fed by gradually being left to themselves. Young children learn to sit quietly in church or to sit up straight in school. Boys develop their courage by doing difficult things. Girls learn how to be friendly by relating with each other and feeling discomfort when they know they have been too familiar or too remote. Some virtues, such as endurance, the ability to concentrate, and readiness to follow instructions, prepare children for schooling.

Those with the experience should recall how this kind of education happens in a traditional Pacific village. Although there are differences from place to place, the lives of village children are carefree and joyful compared to the lives of city children. Yet, they are rarely far from adults—parents, grandparents, uncles and aunties—who guide them in how to act according to custom. They learn when to be exuberant and when to act with respect. They are usually close to any activity, whether it be in the home or in the garden or in the sea, and in time they take on small tasks so as to learn the skills involved and also to develop the endurance that work requires. The little ones largely imitate their elders but gradually learn to do things themselves. Eventually boys will be sent to hunt by themselves. Then there are the stories, told often at night by the old people, and these convey the meanings of the place, the relationships with nature and other persons and an understanding of the things that cannot be done (*tabu*) according to local custom. Religious practice and community, as well, contribute a sense of right and wrong and a grasp of what is ultimate.

Basic Education—Instruction

Aristotle does not go into a great deal of detail about the curriculum for formal schooling, but he does suggest some important directions. The basics are letters, gymnastics, music and drawing. We can take *letters* to include reading, writing and arithmetic, and *drawing* to include geometry and the plastic arts. These subjects are both directly useful in life and preludes to other study. In this sense, the pre-puberty years after age seven are given very much to the basics, so that a fuller curriculum can be anticipated in the later years of formal education.

Gymnastics and sport are directed to the training and strengthening of the body, but here Aristotle makes some important distinctions. In the pre-puberty period, training should not be too hard because it could harm the young body that is growing quickly. In later years, harder training is appropriate and will prepare body and mind for hard work and military service. The character of the training is also important. Aristotle insists that 'the element of nobility, not what is beastlike, should have the leading role'.[5] What he is getting at here is that even sports training involves character formation, so that if children are trained to be savage and rough on the sports field, they will end up this way in later life. Even sports training should teach them to be fine citizens.

Aristotle acknowledges that the curriculum, especially for the later years of formal education is much disputed and that often confusion reigns. There is good reason for this, because the kind of education that is needed will be determined by the kind of life that one wants for the community, and this is often disputed. Communities or parts of communities that are focussed on wealth or on war, or on freedom to do whatever they want, will call for very different forms of education. Aristotle distinguishes between education in things that are useful for life, in things that contribute to virtue and in things that lead to exceptional achievements. Subjects useful to life lead to employment and work. These are surely necessary but they are not the sole end of education. It is around virtue and the particular virtues beneficial for life in particular communities that much disagreement lies. The exceptional achievements are things such as philosophy, the higher sciences and the arts. The point about these subjects is that they are

---

5.   Aristotle, *Politics* VIII, 4 (1338b28), 233.

studied not for their usefulness or economic potential but because they promote the finest exercise of the human mind and sensibility.

These issues are very real for Pacific countries, especially where school curricula tend to be borrowed from larger countries such as Australia, New Zealand and the United States simply because writing curricula and publishing textbooks are very expensive. Adaptation in this case is essential. What are the useful skills for people living in a particular place, and how can a curriculum be designed for the kinds of employment that will be available to them? Are the virtues required for village living the same as those required for city living? Do people destined for chiefly positions require a different education from others and, if so, where will they find it? What higher intellectual and artistic achievements are relevant for a people, and will these include the riches of cultural traditions?

Education for Living Well—The Arts and Culture

It is in his considerations of education in *music* that Aristotle takes us to a higher level. By music, he means not just song and the playing of instruments but also poetry and drama. We might include literature and dance to encapsulate what we would broadly call *the arts*. In some times and places, religious festivals and activities might also be included. Although education in these areas begins in childhood, its fulfilment is found in adulthood, when people freed from having to work for some of the necessities of life and cultivated in the finer things of life are able to enjoy activities not because they are in any way useful but because they are humanly enriching.

Aristotle offers three distinctions that help to position the arts in human life. Life is divided, he says, into work and leisure, into war and peace, and into actions that are useful and actions that are noble. In each of these distinctions, the first item is necessary but it is for the sake of the second. *Work* is a necessary and enduring part of the human condition, but it is for the sake of *leisure*. Leisure should enable the pursuit of *noble* activities. Similarly, citizens need to be capable of going to *war*, if, for instance, it becomes necessary to defend their country, but war is only ever for the sake of *peace*. If these values are to be preserved, education will have to mirror them.

In investigating further, Aristotle finds it necessary to distinguish between leisure and *play*. Play is a part of life and has its place in giving relief from arduous work, but it is merely a kind of relaxation or rest. *Leisure*, for Aristotle, is a more refined and active pursuit that engages with what is best in human life—study of science and philosophy; engagement in the arts. It is for this sense of leisure that Aristotle investigates the place of music in the curriculum. Yet another difference immediately shows up. Music can be used both at play and in leisure, and he makes it clear that he regards different kinds of music differently. The music of play is often noisy and frantic and supplies more sensual kinds of pleasure. We might call it *entertainment*. The music of leisure is more refined and aims at excellence both in performance and in appreciation. It brings its own pleasure, but it is a pleasure that relates to happiness rather than to raw sensuality. We can call this *culture* in the sense of the arts developed by the community.

It is worth asking, what are the sources of this artistically developed culture? For Pacific peoples, there are three broad sources—their own cultural traditions and music, their religion and ritual, and the arts and sciences inherited from the West. These sources are not necessarily in harmony with one another. Some Christian churches tried to suppress traditional religious and other practices. Modern science often seems to contradict traditional accounts of sacred places, and offers descriptions of human life that are in tension with traditional understandings. Elements of Western culture are now themselves undermining Christian religious understandings. Yet all of these sources are important, and consideration should be given to whether and to what extent they can enrich Pacific life. There are judgements to be made about what is true and meaningful. Reconciliation between the sources has also to be achieved, and this is gradually happening, as for instance in the ways that indigenous cultural and religious meanings are being incorporated into Christian ritual.

Although playful entertainment and leisured culture might both find a place in a person's life, the distinction shows up the differences between those members of a community who follow a life of pleasure and those who follow a life of excellence. Under Aristotle's best possible constitution, education would be organised to ensure that those who are citizens are able to find excellence in leisure. Nevertheless whether it is under the best possible constitution, in which all the citizens are cultured and non-citizens labour, or under another constitution, in which only a few follow the life of excellence amidst fellow-citizens who generally follow their pleasures, education in music and the arts has two roles. The first is that it continues the practical education of adults as they learn to be active and fruitful citizens—what Aristotle calls *political education*. The second is that it enables the citizens and the country to live peaceful and fruitful lives—what Aristotle calls *happiness*.

Aristotle gives insight into political education in Book I of his *Ethics*:

> A young man is not a fit person to attend lectures on political science, because he is not versed in the practical business of life from which politics draws its premises and subject-matter. Besides, he tends to follow his feelings, with the result that he will make no headway and derive no benefit from his course, since the object of it is not knowledge but action.[6]

In Aristotle's view, political education takes place after the years of schooling. In the *Politics*, he suggests that people learn to rule by being ruled in the first stage of their adult lives by participating in military activities, which include the activities that we would allocate to police forces, fire brigades and ambulance services. They exercise political roles during middle age, which he takes to be their prime. They retire later in life into religious service. But there is also the management of feelings, and here we return to a discussion of spiritedness. A people needs to be spirited, if it is going to maintain its freedom from domination by other peoples. Yet that same spiritedness, with all its powerful emotions—'fear, pity, indignation, anger, jealousy and love of honour'—can cause havoc when out of control.[7]

In political education, the first role of music or more properly drama and in particular tragedy is that it excites but then *modifies the feelings* of the spirited person. While watching a tragic play, a

---

6. Aristotle, *Ethics* I, 3 (1095a3–6), 6.
7. I am indebted to Carnes Lord, *Education and Culture in the Political Thought of Aristotle* (Ithaca, NY: Cornell University Press, 1982), 164ff. for this reading. Something like half of Book VIII of the *Politics* has been lost and Lord has reconstructed the argument using the *Poetics* and other sources.

person enters into the tragedy and experiences grief and pity and other emotions. As the drama resolves itself members of the audience experience catharsis or a kind of purification, which enables them to balance the workings of these feelings in their lives. The work of art flows back on life and shapes those who appreciate it. There is also another role. The best literature of a culture carries with it the knowledge of the culture, but it does this in a very particular way. It is engaged with universal ideas and principles but is also engaged in the very particulars portrayed in the story. People learn about justice and reconciliation not so much from lectures but by seeing them portrayed in powerful ways. This mix of universal and particular is akin to the virtue of *prudence*, which mediates universal principles and judgements about particular situations. It is, indeed, the virtue of the ruler.

The second role of music and the arts lies in the fulfilment of life, that is, the *achievement of whatever level of happiness is possible* under the conditions in which a people live. Here we can consider both the happiness of the individual person and the happiness of the country. The happiness of a person will be in the life of thoughtful action—public engagement joined to philosophy, science and the arts. The happiness of a country is, however, more circumspect. If a country is primarily directed towards action, it will seek to control its neighbours and hence enter into warfare. If, on the contrary, a country pursues and achieves a life rich in culture and the arts it will be self-sufficient in the fullest sense and will not feel bound to war. The role of education is to draw people towards excellence; the role of the political art is to establish peace and prosperity.

A conundrum arises, however. Under Aristotle's best possible constitution, most citizens will become cultured and virtuous in the sense that we have just examined and the country will also have this character. Under the more likely constitutions, those who achieve real excellence will be a minority. In times of peace and prosperity, therefore, most people will simply follow their pleasures. This is not to say that they will become vicious or wicked. Aristotle talks rather of moral weakness and of softness.[8] Nevertheless, a gulf will open between those seeking amusement and passing pleasures and those who pursue excellence in virtue, thought and the arts. Part of

---

8. See Aristotle, *Ethics* VII.

the pattern of life is that this changes in times of hardship, whether the hardship is brought on by war or famine or disease or natural disaster. Under conditions of hardship, everyone is fully occupied with necessity—pleasure seekers are drawn toward mere survival and the virtuous have little time for leisure. A common condition emerges, which Aristotle calls *endurance*. This explains the strange phenomenon that peoples tend to do well morally and to feel more united with their communities when times are difficult, yet, when times are easy they seem not to make the best of their opportunities.

We have now surveyed the modes of education—habituation, instruction and the flowering of culture. Although they are presented in temporal order and although they are initiated in that order, they are not sharply separated from one another. Habituation begins in infancy, but does not become full virtue until reason and instruction enter in to enable reasoned choice. Habituation continues through the whole of life. Instruction is foreshadowed by childhood stories and is most intense in the years of schooling, but also continues into later life. Music and the arts are begun during school years and include practice in the playing of instruments but reach their fulfilment in adult maturity. Together these modes of education enable the development of human beings who are able to live well and to bring their country to live well.

Excursion Four
Micronesia: The Struggle to Be Chamorro

The Chamorros are the people of the Mariana Islands in north-western Micronesia. Their story illustrates two of Aristotle's senses of the best constitution that we saw in Chapter Three and again in Chapter Five. Under the heading of the best possible arrangement that particular circumstances might *allow*, we have to look at the geography, location and natural resources that a people have available to them. And under the heading of the best possible arrangement that a particular people may be able to *achieve*, we have to look at the history and culture of a people and the ways in which they have learnt to live. The experience of the Chamorros contrasts strongly with that of the Tongans, who have never been colonised and whose history we discussed in Excursion Three. The Chamorros have experienced much intervention, yet they maintain their identity and their culture remains robust.

The Chamorros are descendants of an Austronesian people, probably from the Philippines or Indonesia, who moved through the area and settled in various island groups some three and a half to four thousand years ago. In Micronesia, distances were such that in time those on different island groups developed their own cultures, yet maintained some contact with their distant neighbours. Thus we find the Chamorros distinguished from but sharing similarities with the various communities of the Caroline Islands, the Marshall Islands and Palau. Archaeological evidence also suggests that through the millennia some contact and commerce was maintained with South-East Asia.[1]

---

1. See Scott Russell, *Tiempon I Manmofo'na: Ancient Chamorro Culture and History of the Northern Mariana Islands*, Micronesian Archaeological Survey,

The Chamorros refer to their pre-European-contact ancestors as 'the ancient Chamorros'. Best known is the condition of Chamorro life in the 'latte period', which dated from about AD 1250 till their conquest by the Spanish. It is named for the 'latte stones' that are distinctive of this period and found only in the Marianas. These were pillars that formed the foundations of important houses, and could be four metres high. Each pillar consisted of an upright, on which sat a bowl-shaped capstone. These pillars were quarried out of stone and created impressive structures, which may also have been to a degree earthquake-resistant, due to the possibility of movement between the stones. They are a sign of a strong and vibrant society. The ancient Chamorros grew dry-ground rice and were described by the first Europeans to see them as a big and handsome people. They had developed a wide range of tools, and the speed of their sailing canoes startled the Europeans, who gave them the Malay name, *proa*. They lived in villages with strong hierarchical structures, and kinship lines were matrilineal. War appears to have been regarded as a test of strength. They had and maintain a distinctive language. Present-day Chamorros are showing considerable interest in this history and culture as it relates to their own current situation.[2]

The Mariana Islands consist of fifteen islands extending in two arcs running roughly north-south along the edge of the Mariana Trench in the western Pacific Ocean north of the equator. The four larger islands of the eastern arc (Guam, Rota, Tinian and Saipan)

Report Number 32 (Saipan: CNMI Division of Historic Preservation, 1998), 69–96.

2.   See Don A Farrell, *History of the Mariana Islands to Partition* (Saipan: Public School System of CNMI, 2011). See also his *History of the Northern Mariana Islands* (Saipan: Public School System of CNMI, 1991). While these are school texts, they reflect the high degree of interest that is shown in Chamorro culture. There is also a more academic literature. See, for instance, Michael P Perez, 'Colonialism, Americanization, and Indigenous Identity: A Research Note on Chamorro Identity in Guam', *Sociological Spectrum: Mid-South Sociological Association* 25/5 (2005): 571–91; David Atienza de Frutos and Alexandre Coello de la Rosa, 'Death Rituals and Identity in Contemporary Guam (Mariana Islands)' *Journal of Pacific History* 47/4 (2012): 459–73. See also Jillette Leon-Guerrero, *Seeing Guam through Our Eyes: Prose, Poetry and Imagery Celebrating a Sense of Place* (Agana Heights, Guam: Guamology Publishing, 2010). Popular expression is found in the Guampedia, <http://www.guampedia.com/>, accessed 14 June 2014.

consist of uplifted limestone on top of ancient volcanoes. The islands of the western arc are volcanic and six of the nine have had historic eruptions, the most recent on Anatahan in 2003. This geological formation is caused by the movement of the Pacific Plate under the Philippine Sea Plate.[3] The volcanic islands are steep and rarely populated and then only by small numbers of people. The limestone islands offer flat land, which is reasonably fertile, and ringing reefs, which provide good fishing grounds. The islands are, nevertheless, small. Guam, the largest, is forty-eight kilometres long and six to nineteen kilometres wide with an area of 549 square kilometres. Saipan is just 123 square kilometres in area. The islands sit in a vast sea remote from large countries. Japan is 2600 kilometres to the north, the Philippines 2500 kilometres to the west, Hawaii 6300 kilometres to the east, and California is 9300 kilometres to the north-east.[4] The other islands in their vicinity are also tiny. One could expect that history would have left the Chamorros alone. It was not to be.

The Vagaries of History, Geography and Politics

In 1521, Ferdinand Magellan crossed the Pacific looking for a westerly route to the East Indies. He followed the trade winds, which brought him to Guam on 6 March 1521. It was these same trade winds and the North Equatorial Current along with the geopolitical realities of the day that meant that by 1568 Spanish galleons were sailing annually from Acapulco in Mexico to Cebu in the Philippines and after 1571 to Manila on a route that took them through the Marianas. Guam and Rota, which are four-fifths of the distance across the Pacific, became convenient stopping points where weary sailors could take on supplies of water and fresh food. The return journey took a more northerly route in order to take advantage of different winds, although three Acapulco-bound galleons were damaged by typhoons and wrecked in the Marianas

---

3. See Scott K Rowland et al., 'Anatahan, Northern Mariana Islands: Reconnaissance Geological Observation During and After the Volcanic Crisis of Spring 1990, and Monitoring Prior to the May 2003 Eruption', *Journal of Volcanology and Geothermal Research* 146 (2005): 26–59.
4. <http://www.distancefromto.net/>, accessed 30 July 2014.

in 1568, 1601 and 1638, stranding Spanish and Filipino seamen in the islands.

Although the Spanish had claimed the Marianas in 1565, it was over a hundred years before they showed any inclination to colonise the islands, which had little to offer by way of resources or trade. Then the Jesuit missionary, Fr Diego Luis de San Vitores, petitioned King Philip IV to begin a mission, and on 15 June 1668 a colony was established on Guam. Spain would rule the Marianas for 230 years. At first, the Jesuit priests attempted to assume the role of administrators, but after 1674 secular governors were appointed. The missionaries found some Chamorros who were familiar with European visitors and desirous of contact with them eager for baptism, and the mission was initially successful. However, the Spanish missionary practice of the time called for the people to be turned into Spanish subjects, and when resistance was encountered the military was engaged. In time, disease, conflict and natural disaster saw the Chamorro population reduced from something of the order of 40,000 in 1668 to about 3500 by 1710, and most of them were settled on Guam. In the early nineteenth century, Carolinians were encouraged to settle in the Northern Marianas following natural disasters on their own islands, and Filipinos were brought to work on Guam. Nevertheless, the Spanish did little to develop the islands or to engage the Chamorros in the formal governance of the islands, although they were engaged as organisers of newly formed villages. Under Spanish rule, the Chamorros adopted and adapted Roman Catholicism and many Hispanic customs, but they retained their own language, identity and adaptive culture.[5]

On 20 June 1898, during the three-and-a-half-month Spanish–American War, the American cruiser USS *Charleston* entered Apra Harbor on Guam, and Captain Henry Glass demanded that the astonished Spanish surrender. They did so on the next day, and the *Charleston* sailed on to the Philippines with fifty-six prisoners, the entire Spanish garrison. In the Treaty of Paris signed later that year, Spain ceded the Philippines, Puerto Rico and Guam to the United States for $US20 million. Internationally, this treaty was accepted

---

5. See Robert F Rogers, *Destiny's Landfall: A History of Guam*, revised edition (Honolulu: University of Hawai'i Press, 1995).

as giving the United States sovereignty over Guam. Meanwhile, Spain engaged in negotiations to sell the Northern Marianas, the Caroline Islands and Palau to Germany and did so on 17 November 1899 for the sum of 25 million pesetas. Germany had already claimed the islands and north coast of New Guinea, part of Samoa and the Marshall Islands. Germany administered its possessions lightly, as it was interested mainly in the prestige that came with empire and in the economic benefits that could be gained for German companies, especially through coconut plantations. A generation of Chamorros and Carolinians would, however, be schooled in German, and a people who had been ruled under a single Spanish colonial system would be politically and culturally divided by the interests and actions of new colonial powers.[6]

The American Hold on Guam

American interest in Guam has always been strategic. The Spanish–American War reflected a period of American expansion that also included the acquisition of Hawaii and American Samoa. Initially, Guam was used as a re-coaling station, as was Samoa.[7] Today, it is regarded with the Northern Marianas as the second arc of defence against China and North Korea and as the 'tip of the spear' for any intervention into South-East Asia. The first arc is comprised of defence arrangements with Japan and the Philippines. The northern end of Guam hosts the Andersen Air Force Base, and a large naval base is situated at Apra Harbor, on the west coast. A considerable area of land is dedicated to an armaments depot in the centre of the island, a naval communications installation and a

---

6. See Dirk HR Spennemann, *Edge of Empire: The German Colonial Period in the Northern Mariana Islands*, (Albury, NSW: Heritage Futures, 2007). His *Aurora Australis: The German Period in the Mariana Islands 1899–1914* (Saipan: CNMI Division of Historical Preservation, 1999) offers a picture of what life was like on Saipan during the German period. See also Francis X Hezel, *A Brief Economic History of Micronesia*, Micronesian Seminar, <http://micsem.org/pubs/articles/economic/frames/ecohistfr.htm>, accessed 14 June 2014.

7. Samoa was similarly divided by the colonial powers, leading to today's situation in which American Samoa is an unincorporated unorganised territory of the United States and Samoa (formerly Western Samoa) is an independent state living under a very different political constitution. Culturally the two communities are clearly moving apart.

naval air station. Other land, much of it environmentally degraded, is held in reserve for future military use. In all, the US military holds twenty-seven per cent of the island.[8] In 2013, there were some six thousand military personnel and their families on Guam, but on 3 October of that year a protocol was signed in Tokyo amending the 'Guam International Agreement' and paving the way for a further five thousand military personnel to be moved from Okinawa to Guam.[9]

The people of Guam have never been granted an act of self-determination. The United States holds Guam under Article IV, Section 3 of the US *Constitution*, referred to as the territorial provision. The section covers admission of new states and the United States' powers in regard to territories not yet states. It was intended to cover territories primarily in the west of the continent as they were developed and grew toward statehood. In 1901, a series of Supreme Court cases known collectively as the *Insular Cases* determined under US law that the United States could hold territories (either by treaty or by conquest) that were not slated to become states.[10] Without statehood, these territories lacked the protections of the US *Constitution* in respect of states' powers and were unrepresented in the US Congress. Although regarded as US nationals, their people lacked US citizenship. They were unable to vote in presidential elections, and if they resided in the United States, they were treated as resident aliens. Territories on the way to statehood were called *incorporated territories*; territories intended to remain outside the *Constitution* were called

---

8. See 'Guam' at globalsecurity.org: <http://www.globalsecurity.org/military/facility/guam.htm>; accessed 30 July 2014.

9. See Frank Quimby, 'Fortress Guahan: Chamorro Nationalism, Regional Economic Integration and US Defence Interests Shape Guam's Recent History', *Journal of Pacific History* 46/3 (December 2011): 357–80. Quimby quotes Vice-Admiral George D Murray saying in 1945, 'Military control of these islands is essential . . . The economic development and administration of relatively few native inhabitants should be subordinate to the real purpose for which these islands are held'. See also Gon Namkung and Sulhyung Lee, 'US Power Penetration through the Military Bases in Guam', *Journal of International and Area Studies* 19/2 (2012): 29–46.

10. One curious but advantageous outcome of the *Insular Cases* is that although federal taxes are collected in these territories, they are dedicated solely to the use of the territories themselves.

unincorporated territories. A further distinction was made when unincorporated territories were given a degree of self-government under an 'organic act' of Congress, a kind of quasi-constitution always subject to the will of the US Congress. These territories were called 'organic'. Organic or inorganic, unincorporated territories are nevertheless colonies that are governed by a legislature and executive in respect of which they lack a direct vote and have only limited voice.[11]

As early as 1901, a group of prominent Chamorros presented a petition to the American Government requesting some form of self-government. The US Senate did respond with a Bill meeting some of their requests, but it was left to languish in the House of Representatives. This began a long series of rebuffs. Henry Kissinger was quoted as saying of the whole of Micronesia, 'There are only 90,000 people out there. Who gives a damn?'[12] The military resisted any moves that would complicate their operations, and, apart from the Japanese occupation during World War II, Guam was governed by a series of naval officers until 1950. Governance was usually remiss, as the island was dependent on appropriations by Congress, and these were generally meagre and quickly used for military purposes. On 1 August 1950, after five years of lobbying by Guam leaders and a walkout by the Guam Congress, President Truman signed the *Organic Act of Guam* into law, and this gave the people of Guam a degree of self-government with American-style institutions.[13] They were also granted American citizenship and later

11. See Ediberto Román and Theron Simmons, 'Membership Denied: Subordination and Subjugation under United States Expansionism', *San Diego Law Review* 39/437 (2002): 437–524. As we shall see, an organised unincorporated territory has limited home rule and elects a 'delegate' to the US Congress. That delegate cannot vote on the House Floor, but can vote in committee and in caucus.
12. Quoted by Román and Simmons, 'Membership Denied', 500. Similar statements by prominent politicians and military officers abound. The US Navy had an interest in assuring that the people of Guam did not become citizens, as this would have allowed them to seek remedies for appropriated property and for other inconveniences. See Timothy P Maga, 'The Citizenship Movement in Guam, 1946–1950', *Pacific Historical Review* 53/1 (February 1984): 59–77.
13. *The Organic Act of Guam and Related Federal Laws Affecting the Governmental Structure of Guam* can be found at <http://www.guamcourts.org/compileroflaws/GCA/OrganicAct/Organic%20Act.PDF>; accessed 20 July 2014.

a non-voting representative in Congress. Federal administration of the territory was moved from the US Navy to the Department of the Interior. Guam is today an organised unincorporated territory of the United States.[14]

The problem for the people of Guam is that although in comparison to many Pacific island countries they enjoy a high material standard of living, much of which flows from work associated with the military bases, they are still not strictly in charge of their own destiny. To the Pacific traveller, Guam presents a shock. Its six-lane Marine Corps Drive on the west coast and its attendant businesses could be anywhere in mainland United States, but it is still a tiny island with an indigenous population that clings to its culture. In the epilogue to *Destiny's Landfall: A History of Guam*, Robert F Rogers urges a compromise between the interests of Guam and the interests of the United States that would end Guam's colonial status. He says:

> That compromise should be met as both a moral imperative and as a practical necessity because—as this history demonstrates—colonialism fosters cultures of corruption. The imposition of alien values, whether in the name of religion, commerce, military necessity or democracy, on other cultures is one of the most corrosive aspects of colonialism. This corrosion degrades not only the colonial subjects but also erodes the moral integrity of the colonial power. Such has been the case of United States rule on Guam.[15]

---

14. Howard P Willens and Dirk A Ballendorf, in *The Secret Guam Study* (Saipan: Micronesian Area Research Centre and NMI Division of Historic Preservation, 2004), show how as late as 1975 a study commissioned by President Ford was made secret and buried by the bureaucracy after it advocated a form of commonwealth to be determined by the people of Guam in consultation with the President. It also proposed that the political arrangements for Guam be at least as advantageous as those enjoyed by the Commonwealth of the Northern Marianas. To date, this has not happened.

15. Rogers, *Destiny's Landfall*, 286.

Japan in the Northern Marianas

With the outbreak of World War I in 1914, Japan seized the German possessions in Micronesia with the secret consent of Britain and its European allies but without consulting the United States. The territory included all of Micronesia, except Guam and the Gilbert Islands (Kiribati) and Nauru, which were British possessions. The Japanese occupation was swift, efficient and disciplined but also respectful of local customs and practice. Having installed a naval administration, the Japanese set up administrative centres on the main islands and encouraged economic development, assisted by already long-term Japanese residents. Such was the manner of their occupation that at the end of the war European powers looked favourably on their continued presence. Japan would have preferred to annex the islands, but American President Woodrow Wilson was opposed to it. The compromise in the 1919 negotiations among the victors was a League of Nations Mandate under which Japan would establish its own system of law, be banned from building fortifications and be obliged to allow free commerce and trade. After 1922, the Japanese Navy withdrew, and the islands came under Japanese civilian administration. Their rule was intense and very competent and gradually established Japanese ways in the islands. They worked to establish industries that would support the Japanese homeland and make the islands self-sufficient.[16]

On Saipan, Matsue Haruji, who had studied agriculture at Louisiana State University, established his South Seas Development Company (NKK) and generated a thriving sugar cane industry with the support of the Japanese Imperial Navy, which purchased all of the product. Sugar farming took up much of the flat land on the island and then expanded onto the island of Tinian. The industry was dependent on immigrant labour, and by the mid-1930s forty-five thousand Japanese farmers from Okinawa far outnumbered the three thousand Chamorros and Carolinians.[17] By the outbreak of the Pacific War in 1941, Saipan's population was of the order of

---

16. See Mark R Peattie, *Nan'yō: The Rise and Fall of the Japanese in Micronesia 1885–1945*, Pacific Islands Monograph Series, Number 4 (Honolulu: University of Hawai'i Press, 1988).
17. Peattie, *Nan'yō*, 123–32, 157–69.

100,000, a significant number of whom were Korean. Although excluded from government, the Chamorros were allowed to maintain their own customs and witnessed a period of economic prosperity driven by high levels of temporary immigration. Two generations of Chamorros were schooled in Japanese. This would have fateful consequences, for, when the Japanese occupied Guam, they used Chamorro interpreters from the Northern Marianas. Some of these would come to be regarded by the Chamorros of Guam as collaborators.[18]

The Problem of Micronesia

World War II came to the Pacific on the morning of 7 December 1941 with the Japanese attack on the US fleet at Pearl Harbor in Hawaii. Just a few hours later, Japanese aircraft from Saipan assisted by carrier-based aircraft began bombing Guam. On 10 December, some five thousand Japanese soldiers landed on Guam and quickly overran the tiny American garrison of largely Chamorro militia. Under military rule, life on Saipan became harsh; on Guam it was punitive. American forces took the islands from the Japanese in 1944 in attacks that began with days of extensive naval and aerial bombardment, which destroyed much of the infrastructure of the islands. The Battle of Saipan (18 June–9 July) was one of the fiercest of the war and saw 30,000 Japanese soldiers killed. One of the marked tragedies of the war was the suicide of thousands of Japanese civilians, who jumped from the northern cliffs of Saipan to avoid capture. In the Battle of Guam (21 July–10 August) virtually all of the Japanese garrison of 18,500 were killed. Many Chamorros were killed or injured; most survived by hiding in limestone caves.

By the end of the war, the United States had regained Guam and had occupied all of the former Japanese-held parts of Micronesia. The problem was what to do with them. There was an inclination

---

18. See Jose S Dela Cruz, *From Colonialism to Self-Government: The Northern Marianas Experience* (Honolulu: Scripta, 2010), 92–9. See also Keith L Comacho, 'The Politics of Indigenous Collaboration: The Role of Chamorro Interpreters in Japan's Pacific Empire, 1914–45', *Journal of Pacific History* 43/2 (September 2008): 207–22.

on the part of the American Government to annex all of the islands as US territory, but the international mood was against this. After some negotiation, the United States accepted responsibility for the Trust Territory of the Pacific Islands on 18 July 1947.[19] It was a 'strategic' trust, a new invention in law that allowed the United States to maintain a military presence. The United States was obliged under the trust to promote the economic, social and political development of the people and to prepare them for their future political status. Lacking clear direction from Washington about the future of the islands, the US administration of the Trust Territory of the Pacific Islands became a 'holding action', and many of the islands reverted to a subsistence economy. However, by the early 1960s the international decolonisation movement was growing and in 1964 the US Department of the Interior created the territory-wide Congress of Micronesia as a first step towards self-government and self-determination. In 1968, the Congress formed a Political Status Commission. The expectation of the United Nations and of the United States was that a united Micronesia would choose either affiliation with the United States or independence.[20]

This began a vigorous process, and in 1970 the Congress of Micronesia declared four principles: sovereignty of the people, the right of self-determination, the right to form and amend their constitution, and the intention of free association that could be terminated by either party. Carl Heine, a Marshallese, was party to the deliberations and put a case for a united Micronesia in free association with the United States in his book, *Micronesia at the Crossroads*. He was scathing about how colonial powers had treated the region:

---

19. Guam was left out of the Trust Territory and, therefore, was later not party to the Congress of Micronesia. 'Micronesia' took a different meaning, a political meaning, which excluded Kiribati and Nauru, which were geographically part of Micronesia. Guam's position became ambiguous.

20. See Howard P Willens and Deanne C Siemer, *An Honorable Accord: The Covenant between the Northern Mariana Islands and the United States*, Pacific Islands Monographs Series, Number 18 (Honolulu: University of Hawai'i Press, 2002), chapter 1.

Spain ruled under the influence of medieval Catholicism. Germany was guided largely by economic imperialism. Japan's objectives were military and economic expansion. The United States' administration amounts to apathetic paternalism with strategic military considerations.[21]

There were tensions between the desire for traditional forms of life and the desire to embrace modernity. Questions were raised about how the six districts, with their different languages and separated by vast distances, could unite. In the event, the Northern Marianas broke away from the rest and declared that it wanted a closer relationship with the United States, a decision the Chamorros had made as far back as 1951. In 1976 they became an unincorporated commonwealth within the United States as defined by a negotiated covenant, a more advantageous arrangement than that enjoyed by Guam.[22] The rest of Micronesia split into independent republics, each with a negotiated agreement of free association with the United States—the Republic of Palau, the Federated States of Micronesia (Yap, Chuuk, Pohnpei and Kosrae) and the Republic of the Marshall Islands. The UN Trust was formally dissolved in 1986 and the people of the Commonwealth of the Northern Mariana Islands (CNMI) became US citizens. The trusteeship for Palau did not end until 1992.[23]

The path of the CNMI has been rocky. Its first attempts to unite with Guam were rebuffed in a plebiscite on Guam, and so it set out to make the best of the advantages it had. Two of these under the *Covenant* were control of its own immigration laws and exemption from US minimum wage law until such time as the US Congress

---

21. Carl Heine, *Micronesia at the Crossroads: A Reappraisal of the Micronesian Political Dilemma* (Canberra: ANU Press, 1974), 10.

22. The *Covenant to Establish a Commonwealth of the Northern Marianas Islands in Political Union with the United States of America* is reproduced in Willens and Siemer, *An Honorable Accord*, appendix. It is also available online at <http://www.cnmilaw.org/cnmicovenant.html>; accessed 30 July 2014.

23. See Lizabeth A McKibben, 'The Political Relationship between the United States and Pacific Islands Entities: The Path to Self-Government in the Northern Mariana Islands, Palau, and Guam', *Harvard International Law Journal* 31/1 (Winter 1990): 257–93. See also Larry Wentworth, 'The International Status and Personality of Micronesian Political Entities', *ILSA Journal of International Law* 16/1 (1993): 1–37; and David Hanlon, *Remaking Micronesia: Discourses over Development in Pacific Territory 1944–1982* (Honolulu: University of Hawai'i Press, 1998).

decided to impose specific laws. These advantages and CNMI's proximity to Asia gave birth to the clothing industry, in which immigrant South-East Asian workers were granted temporary visas to work for better wages than they would have received in their own countries to produce clothes cheaply that could be labelled 'Made in America' and exported without quotas into mainland United States. Proximity to Asia, relaxed immigration laws and the beauty of the islands also gave rise to a vibrant tourist industry. Now, the clothing industry has collapsed and the factories are derelict. It was a fickle industry, and the World Trade Organization deregulation of clothing import quotas made Saipan's clothing industry redundant. As well, CNMI did not have the capacity to properly regulate the industry, which allowed abuse of workers, which, in turn, infuriated the US Congress, which began limiting CNMI powers. The tourist industry also faced major setbacks brought on by the Asian Economic Crisis in 1997, airline deregulation, increases in the cost of fuel, reduced flights and the reduction in foreign travel after the 2001 terrorist attacks in the United States. Between 1998 and 2008, government revenue declined from $US248 million to $US156 million. Battles about access to foreign workers and the imposition of federal minimum wage rates are ongoing with the US Congress as the CNMI tries to work out its future.[24]

The Chamorros

With this history of intervention, war and immigration, it may seem surprising that Chamorro culture and identity have survived, but they have. Table Two provides a breakdown of the populations of Guam and CNMI by ethnicity. In July 2015, the Chamorros

---

24. See Frank Quimby, 'Americanised, Decolonised, Globalised and Federalised', *Journal of Pacific History* 48/4 (2013): 464–83. For more general accounts of this history, see Dela Cruz, *From Colonialism to Self-Government*, chapters 33–43; Willens and Siemer, *An Honorable Accord*, chapter 10. The tense relations between the CNMI and the US Congress on immigration and the federal minimum wage can be charted in annual reviews by Samuel F McPhetres, 'Micronesia in Review: Northern Mariana Islands', in *Contemporary Pacific*, 1999–2014. For the impact of American paranoia after the terrorist attacks on the United States in 2001, see Keith L Camacho, 'After 9/11: Militarized Borders and Social Movements in the Mariana Islands', *American Quarterly* 64/4 (December 2012): 685–713.

constituted 37.3 per cent (60,346) of the population of Guam and 23.9 per cent (12,510) of the population of CNMI.[25] A further 58,240 Chamorros live on the US mainland. In the southern parts of Guam, villages are clearly Chamorro communities.[26]

Table Two. Comparative data on the populations of Guam and CNMI, July 2015

	Guam	CNMI
Chamorro	60,346 37.3%	12,510 23.9%
Carolinian	few specified	4.6%
Pacific Islander	12.0%	6.4%
Filipino	26.3%	35.3%
Asian/ other Asian	7.3%	14.7%
White	7.1%	few specified
Mixed	9.4%	12.7%
Other	0.6%	2.5%
Estimated total population (100%)	161,785	52,344

This resilience is explained in part by the fact that Chamorro society is matrilineal and matrifocal. As *matrilineal*, kinship is traced through women and traditionally ownership of land and other property has also been passed down through female lines. This has endured despite American attempts since 1898 to enforce patrilineal institutions, indicated by Chamorro surnames. As *matrifocal*, the Chamorro culture is mother-centred. The mothers hold central place in extended families and are responsible for socialisation, language, education and religious ritual. They exercise considerable authority in both family and community. After conversion to Catholicism under the Spanish they readily

---

25. Data for Table Two sourced from CIA, *World Fact Book*, <https://www.cia.gov/ library/publications/the-world-factbook/>, accessed 1 September 2015. The CNMI column accurately reproduces the small rounding error of 0.1% present in the CIA data.

26. 2000 census. See Fay F Untalan, 'Chamorro Migration to the US', Guampedia, <http://www.guampedia.com/chamorro-migration-to-the-u-s/>, accessed 30 July 2014.

adopted devotions to the Blessed Virgin Mary, which have become central to the culture. Even with the advent of modern medicine, traditional practices are maintained around birth, and women play a major role in funeral rites, which have their own distinctive features.[27] Another aspect of Chamorro resilience is their readiness to welcome outsiders into their families. As Spanish, Filipino, German, Japanese and American immigrants, usually male, have married Chamorros, they have been incorporated into families and their children have been raised as Chamorros.[28]

The Chamorro core values attributed to the ancient Chamorros and taught to children today are interdependence, reciprocity and respect for rank, age and nature. There is every reason to believe that these values, which we might call virtues, are still central to Chamorro life. They lead to practices such as decision-making by consensus, co-operation and generosity among extended families and a practice of gift-giving or donation, which is reciprocated.[29] Such a culture is necessarily going to find itself at odds with American culture, in which the individual is paramount, economics aggressive and politics conflictual. This is the dilemma that Chamorros face, and it is made more difficult by the adoption of American political institutions, which carry American culture with them.[30]

In Chapter Six we defined *culture* as 'the learning that a people has achieved with respect to living in a certain way in a certain place and with particular neighbours'. Anthropologist Gerald

---

27. See Laura Marie Torres Souder, *Daughters of the Island: Contemporary Chamorro Women Organizers on Guam*, Micronesian Area Research Centre Monograph Series, Number 1 (Lanham, MD: University Press of America, 1992), chapter 3, pages 43–77. See also David Atienza de Frutos and Alexandre Coello De La Rosa, 'Death Rituals and Identity in Contemporary Guam (Mariana Islands)', *Journal of Pacific History* 47/4 (December 2012): 459–73; and Anne Perez Hattori, ' "The Cry of the Little People of Guam": American Colonialism, Medical Philanthropy, and the Susan Hospital for Chamorro Women, 1898–1941', *Health and History* 8/1 (2014): 4–26.
28. See Ann M Pobutsky, 'Economics and Fertility' *History of the Family* 6/1 (2001): 95–123.
29. *Chamorro Heritage: A Sense of Place; Guidelines and Recommendations for Authenticating Chamorro Heritage* (Guam: Department of Chamorro Affairs, 2003), 23–9. See also Lawrence J. Cunningham, *Ancient Chamorro Society* (Honolulu: Bess Press, 1992), 83–96.
30. See Michael P Perez, 'Pacific Identities beyond US Racial Formations: The Case of Chamorro Ambivalence and Flux', *Social Identities: Journal for the Study of Race, Nation and Culture* 8/3 (2002): 457–79.

Arbuckle criticises early anthropological definitions of culture and generates his own in the light of more recent developments in the discipline. An early definition saw culture as that 'complex whole which includes knowledge, belief, art, morals, law, custom, and any other capabilities and habits acquired by man as a member of society'.[31] Arbuckle's criticism is that this definition is too static and, as used by anthropologists, has implied that 'primitive' or pure cultures would not change, though, of course, they could be destroyed. Indeed, culture has sometimes been idealised as something that should not change. Twentieth-century criticism has recognised, on the other hand, that cultures do change, that people in them are agents of change, that symbols are interpreted and reinterpreted and that cultures undergo periods of chaos. Arbuckle provides his own definition:

> Culture is a pattern of meanings encased in a network of symbols, myths, narratives and rituals; created by individuals and subdivisions, as they struggle to respond to the competitive pressures of power and limited resources in a rapidly globalising and fragmenting world; and instructing its adherents about what is considered to be the correct way to feel, think, and behave.[32]

He could add that culture is dynamic, and it changes; it is, nevertheless, tough; it seeks to endure. This is the story of the Chamorros, who have managed to adapt to the impact of Western intervention on their lives. While this has led to times of chaos, there is no reason to believe that such a condition should be permanent. The Chamorros may well be living through another period of very great change, but in the end their challenge is to learn how to live successfully on very small islands in a vast ocean with large and powerful neighbours, who from time to time are inclined to meddle in their affairs.[33]

---

31. Edward Tylor, *Primitive Culture*, volume 1 (New York: Harper, 1871), 1. Quoted by Gerald A Arbuckle, *Culture, Inculturation, and Theologians: A Postmodern Critique* (Collegeville, MN: Liturgical Press, 2010), 2.
32. Arbuckle, *Culture, Inculturation, and Theologians*, 17.
33. Roger Keesing argues that culture has different facets, constructive and destructive, and that the latter need to be changed. See Roger M Keesing, 'Creating the Past: Custom and Identity in the Contemporary Pacific', *Contemporary Pacific* 1/1–2 (1989): 19–42.

Chapter Nine
Sustaining Political Life—Business and Wealth

Neither human beings nor whole countries can survive without proper sustenance. At the first level, this means food, clothing and shelter, though as communities become more complex, their needs for material things become greater. The modern world relies on far more products than Aristotle would ever have imagined, though the basics are still the same, even if they are supplied in very different ways. Here we touch into that side of humanity that is animal, a material living being that comes to be by nature and is supplied with its needs by nature, particularly by the earth itself.

The study of how these materials are supplied and managed is *economics* and today involves many other sciences, such as agricultural science and marine science. Aristotle tells us that economic science is prior in origin to political science, because the survival of the household is prior to the formation of the political community. Much of what economics tells us is, therefore, beyond the scope of this book. Politics, however, is prior in the order of ends and so will be responsible for thinking about how economic activities enter into the life of a community and about how they are so ordered that the people will live well. The political community as a whole also needs certain materials, if it is to function well.

It is in this context that we will now discuss issues to do with wealth and business. The first section of this chapter will examine wealth and property. The second section will look at business and taxation. The third section will raise certain ethical concerns that surround business and wealth.

Possessions, Land and Money

The *possessions* that are first and absolutely essential are food, clothing and shelter. Aristotle notes that among the animals different species are formed according to the ways in which they find food, and the kind of food they eat will determine how they live—in small groups or large groups, together or spread out. Sea birds, for instance, eat only fish and spread out over vast areas of sea, while scrub birds eat insects in the leaf litter and live in small groups. Small seed-eating birds fly short distances but mostly in the cover of trees and shrubs and tend to live in flocks. Animals do not change very much and, if their particular food source disappears, they do not survive. On the other hand, human beings adapt to different circumstances without becoming different species, but have very different kinds of lives due to the different ways in which they find their food, shelter and clothing. Lives can be built around hunting or grazing or fishing or agriculture or around a mix of these, and this reminds us that life is dependent on the earth and the sea. In more complex communities, people can be more remote from the earth and supply their needs by commerce, as happens in large modern cities, where people may never see food growing, and children may even think that fish is made in cans. Yet, the dependence on land and sea remains.

The possessions that follow are the instruments or tools that support the kinds of lives that we live. They may be the tools that help in food production, house building and the making of clothes. Other tools, such as furniture, make life more comfortable. Still others allow us to do things that we enjoy, such as travel, whether it be by horse or by bicycle or by motor vehicle. Musical instruments enable us to express our creativity and to enjoy beautiful sounds. As communities grow, larger and more sophisticated instruments are needed, such as good roads, sewerage systems and piped water supplies. It is in regard to these sorts of possessions that Aristotle begins to talk about *wealth*. Someone who has a truly adequate supply of useful instruments is wealthy; someone who has less than they really need is poor. However, what it is to be rich or poor will vary between different places, because what is needed for different kinds of lives will not be the same.

The distribution of *land* is often a difficult issue. Ideally, the extent of a country's territory is clear and the people in it are united and agreed in their ownership of it. Should there be difficulties with neighbouring peoples, the question of war or of how to prevent war arises. The big question, however, is how the land should be divided and who should own what or how much. Aristotle surveys some common views in Book II of the *Politics*, and we shall return shortly to some of the principles he discerns. In Book VII, while discussing his best possible constitution, he suggests that the land should be divided in two, with one part given to common ownership of the whole community and the other part given to private ownership. Further, the common part should again be divided so that one part is used to provide for the expenses in religious matters and the other part is used to provide for the remaining general expenses of the whole community. The part given to private ownership should be divided into a part close to the city and a part on the boundary of the country, and individuals should be given one allotment in each part.

Aristotle is not here suggesting an exact mathematical division but rather establishing some principles. A country does need common land, for its cities and public facilities, for its churches and schools and in order to generate the wealth that it needs for its public activities. Private land needs to be shared somewhat evenly so that all prosper, but the advantages and disadvantages of different kinds of land should also be taken into account. In his example, it is advantageous to live near the city, with its activities and markets, and disadvantageous to live near the frontiers, where one is more likely to be subject to attacks by other people. Although he sees an advantage in each citizen having a similar amount of land, because they will be less likely to become jealous of one another, he thinks it unnecessary to enforce this by law, and he recognises that some will by cleverness and diligence always be richer than others. He does, however, see an important connection between land and population. If land is limited, the population should be limited to the number of people that the land can support.

Nevertheless, he recognises that the issues are difficult. 'For the nature of desire is without limit, and it is with a view to satisfying this that many live.'[1] His solution is a political one. Those who are virtuous should be educated to want no more than they need, and those who are not virtuous and desire too much should be restrained by law. In fact, most places have customs and laws about land ownership that

---

1. Aristotle, *Politics* II, 7 (1267b1), 69.

are fairly stable, but he points out that if things get out of balance revolutions can happen or rulers may need to step in and bring about some sort of redistribution.

One of the questions that arises about land is whether it should be owned privately or communally. It is really a question about wealth generally, which includes food, animals, material possessions and money, but it is about land that it is often most pressing. Aristotle argues that ownership should be private, because this prevents squabbling and ensures better care of the property, but that the fruits of the property, namely food, possessions and money, should be shared more commonly. The sharing may be simply common, in which case everyone takes food, for instance, from a common storehouse, or it may take place through generosity, in which case those who produce have both the pleasure of owning and the pleasure of sharing the things they produce with others.

The issue of land is often a difficult one in the Pacific, where much land is under customary title and tied to a tribe, clan or family. This is very different from the practice in Western countries, where land is viewed largely as a commodity. Pacific peoples are often told that they should put their land on 'the market'. The issues are not simple. Even in Australia, two people might look at the same piece of land and see different things. A European Australian might simply see 'real estate', something to be sold; an Aboriginal Australian might see country that carries the meaning of the ancestors who have lived on it. Values that see land as more than real estate are important and should be maintained, while at the same time ensuring it is possible for everyone to live well and for the community as a whole to pursue its public activities. In a practical sense, in subsistence economies such as parts of the Pacific land is the only real wealth, because all other needs are supplied by it.

Money is not something natural but comes into being through human agreement or convention. Aristotle places the origin of money in the need to exchange goods with people who are either at a distance or whose items of exchange will be ready at a different time. In simple exchanges people barter one thing for another— vegetables for fruit or shoes for chairs—but money was invented to overcome the difficulties of time, distance and perishability. At first, metals such as gold or silver, which would not corrode, were used, but then they were stamped to indicate the authority of a ruler or government that was guaranteeing their agreed value. In modern times, we have introduced printed paper and plastic notes and even monetary wealth that consists of little more than numbers in a computer. The underlying principle remains the same, namely, that these instruments of exchange carry an agreed value and that they will be recognised by everyone who acts in the markets where they are accepted. Other more recently invented financial instruments are more confusing and carry only a market value, which is based on confidence in the markets and is heavily influenced by greed and fear and which can collapse, sometimes for no apparent reason.

Each of the things we have discussed—food and shelter, the material goods that make life easier, land and money—is a part of what constitutes wealth. What is most fundamental are the things that make life possible—food, shelter and tools—yet people tend to measure wealth solely in terms of money. Money, however, is a strange thing. One cannot eat it or sleep on it, and it only shows its value when it is transferred to another person in exchange for something else. In fact, what people need will differ from place to place. A person living at the top of a tall building in the middle of a large city will need plenty of money and expensive tools, such as elevators. Persons living on their own land in a good environment will have much of what they need to live and be able to do with much less money and fewer machines. In this sense, Pacific countries do very well. It has often been said that no one is poor or need be poor in the Pacific, because everyone has land and family and with work can have adequate food and shelter. On the other hand, people in Pacific countries often expect their relatives in countries such as Australia, New Zealand and the United States to send them money. It is true that people in those countries usually have more money, but it is often forgotten that in those economies they need more in order to live. Still, the problem for Pacific peoples is how to obtain things that are more readily available in the larger countries, such as high quality medical care or large machinery.

Household Management, Business and Taxation

Aristotle distinguishes between a household and its management, and a business and its management. By a *household* he means much more than a husband and wife and some children. His household is the basic unit of human life and of the production of wealth. It is, perhaps, best thought of as an extended family living on agricultural land together with servants or employees, who are engaged in farming and in the various crafts that keep life going. The principles worked out for this arrangement, however, can be applied as is appropriate to other kinds of household, even those that are much smaller. There are two aspects to household management—the management of people and the management of wealth.

The *first relationship* in the household is that between husband and wife. It is a partnership necessary by nature for the continuation of human life but necessary also because of the complementary gifts a man and a woman contribute to life together. Aristotle clearly believes that the husband should rule the household for the sake of its order and protection but that the relationship of man and wife is political and therefore participatory on both sides. A husband should never harm his wife, and the wife should manage her own domain—the relationships and internal activities of the family—in her own right with the delicacy, gentleness and resourcefulness that her husband could not manage. Some of the things she knows, she should not tell her husband. This view is, of course, at odds with the modern Western view that puts liberty and equality first and that from the political perspective sees all men and all women as indistinguishably the same.[2] There is room for discussion among Pacific peoples about how the complex relationships within extended families and between men and women are best understood and lived.

The *productive relationship* of the household is between master and servant, which is in many respects close to what we know as the relationship between manager and employee. This is an essentially different kind of relationship because of the difference in capacity between master and servant and because of the kind of activity that is involved. The role of the master is to look ahead, to plan and to know what to do. The role of the servant is to carry out the work. The activity that has to do with generating necessary perishables such as food has to be done continuously and on time and so is not open to political negotiation. Aristotle calls this *labour*.

---

2. The Western liberal view was pioneered by John Locke and its roots can be found in his *Second Treatise of Civil Government*, chapter VI.

Aristotle suggests four roles for the householder in relation to wealth—acquiring it, guarding it, keeping it in order and making proper use of it. Each of these has many parts and demands its own skills, which are learnt through being brought up in the household and through schooling and experience. The household will be engaged in exchange or trade for the sake of acquiring those goods that it cannot grow or make itself. At the first level, this may be by simple exchange of goods, but money might also be used. A change comes when this exchange is done not for the sake of supplying household necessities but for the sake of creating further wealth. We call this *business*, and it can apply to all areas of productive work. A Tongan talking-chief expressed this difference to me in these words: 'Here we don't call it farming; we call it providing for your family'.[3]

Aristotle distinguishes two kinds of business, which we can call productive and commercial. *Productive business* is engaged in making food or artefacts that people need and are willing to buy. It increases wealth but is limited in that what is made must be actually needed and useful, so that people will buy it. *Commercial business* is engaged in selling what other people have produced. It is a necessary activity, particularly when products come from a distance or need to be sold at a distance. In a sense, commercial activity is a service both to producers and consumers. But Aristotle notes that this kind of activity does not produce anything but rather generates wealth based on money through the exchange of goods that some other business has produced. For instance, a storekeeper uses money to buy things that someone else has made and sells them on to users for a price that includes his costs but also a profit that is added. The business can expand both in terms of the number of products sold and in terms of the number of customers reached. There is a sense in which the wealth it produces can increase without limit.

In the modern world, the use of this kind of wealth has been taken much further, so that money-wealth itself generates wealth, sometimes without any obvious connection to productive activity. Even in the area of productive activity, the means of production, such as factories or mines or large farms or plantations, have become so big and expensive, that it has become essential to gather and protect vast sums of money for building and maintaining these businesses. We

3. Conversation with Telenisi, Ha'apai, Tonga, 2005.

call this *capital*, and it is a form of wealth that is even more removed from the early senses of wealth such as food and other perishable necessities that are readily shared whenever they are available in abundance. Money in this sense is not for easy spending but needs to be managed carefully and to be used only where it will effectively lead to the generation of new wealth.

People in Pacific countries often have difficulty establishing productive businesses. They are extremely good at producing food and basic necessities at the level of the household, but in a globalised world in which processed food and household goods are manufactured cheaply in large factories and shipped around the world, they find it difficult to compete. There are good reasons for this. The islands are small with small populations and so have small workforces and small markets; countries lack and have difficulty generating the large quantities of capital wealth necessary to build factories; customs incline people away from work that must continue twenty-four hours a day and 365 days a year. Nevertheless, there are successful productive businesses in the Pacific islands, usually on a small scale. In every country, it can be asked, what are the things we import, and how could we make alternatives simply and cheaply? For instance, it makes little sense to import potato chips from around the world when breadfruit chips can be made by a household industry. Another strategy is to ask, what have we that other people might value? There is, for instance, discussion in Palau about whether the people there should exclude foreign commercial fishing from their economic zone in order to encourage tourism and recreational fishing, which could generate more income for the country.

Just as the household requires wealth so that people can live well, so does the political community or country as a whole. Governments are not usually engaged in either productive or commercial business, and are often unsuccessful when they try. Instead, governments receive the wealth they need to protect the country and to provide services for the whole community through *taxation*. It simply means that people living in a country contribute a portion of their personal or communal wealth to the country as a whole, so that it can function well. In the modern world, taxation is generally through money and may be a tax on income or land or exchange. In non-cash economies, it need not be in money but might be in service or land or products of the land. There are many methods of taxation, but what is essential is that a portion of the wealth held by individuals and businesses be contributed to the country as a whole.

Ethical Concerns

Before leaving the topic of business and wealth, we will note three areas of ethical concern around the topic of business and wealth that are worthy of continuing reflection. The first has to do with the kind of justice that belongs to business activity and its relationship to other forms of justice. The second has to do with human relations in business and in the productive activities of the household. The third raises the question of whether there are moral limits to how much wealth we should have.[4]

How is *justice* exercised in business? The conception of justice that functions in business flows from the kind of activity that business is. The commercial side of business is about trade and exchange, which are necessarily done in relationship with other people. If one does not tell the truth about one's product and the other party realises that it has bought something that is not of the standard it appeared to be, that party will complain of unfairness, and the relationship will fail. Similarly, in business, the terms of exchange are negotiated and contracts are made. Prices are set not by law but by agreement related to demand. Should one receive what is owed under a contract but not give what is owed in return, again the relationship will fail. Reflecting on these things, Plato defined justice in the context of business as 'speaking the truth and paying your debts'.[5]

Aristotle calls this kind of justice *commutative justice*, and it applies whenever two people enter into a contract or agreement. However, it

---

4. I have dealt with these questions at much greater length in three articles: 'Plato and Aristotle on the Ethics of Business', *Philosophy for Business*, number 54, 19 October 2009; 'Aristotle on the Ethics of Workplace Relations', *Philosophy for Business*, number 55, 4 December 2009; 'Aristotle and Locke on the Moral Limits of Wealth', *Philosophy for Business*, number 59, 28 April 2010. *Philosophy for Business* is available at <http://www.isfp.co.uk/businesspathways/>, accessed 1 August 2014.
5. Plato, *The Republic*, in *The Collected Dialogues of Plato*, edited by Edith Hamilton and Huntington Cairns (Princeton: Princeton University Press, 1961) Book I, 331c–d, 580.

differs from *distributive justice*, which is the kind of justice that looks to the fairness of the distribution of common goods, such as 'honour or money or such other assets as are divisible among members of the community'.[6] It is the responsibility of leaders of communities and governments of countries to ensure that wealth, recognition and participation are shared fairly across the community. These two kinds of justice can readily come into conflict. In Pacific countries, it is often difficult to keep a business going because family members approach its assets with a notion of distributive justice. They feel that because they are in need and a relative appears to have money, the money should be shared. When this happens, capital is lost, and the business is unable to enter into new contracts to purchase things to sell. Often it will collapse. In large industrialised countries, companies can be so large that they skew the fair distribution of wealth but claim that they are responsible only to the markets, to shareholders and to the contracts they have made.

Our second concern is with human relationships within the productive side of business—what today we call *workplace relations*. In his discussion of relationships within the household, Aristotle notes three factors that affect the relationship between master and servant or, for us, employer and employee. First, human survival is dependent on the fruits of the earth, which are perishable, so that human labour is constant. Food rots if it is stored too long and so must be grown all the time. Similarly, financial capital is depleted if the activities it funds do not keep earning. Production and therefore the labour that supports it cannot stop. Secondly, human beings have different capacities and this puts them into unequal relationships with one another, such as in the employer–employee relationship. Thirdly, some people, especially those who are strong and spirited, desire to dominate others, and may well be successful if others lack these qualities.

The consequence of these factors is that the relationships in productive business are not political in the sense that everyone participates in decision-making and leadership, nor in the sense that some form of consensus is necessary before activity takes place. Rather, they are built around the imperative to keep work going and for those who labour to do what they are told to do. The risk that

---

6. Aristotle, *Ethics* V, 2 (1130b32), 118.

Aristotle sees in this situation is that employees will be reduced to a condition of slavery. The ethical imperative, therefore, is to inject forms of respect for human beings into the workplace, so that even when the pressures on business to perform are great and the work itself is arduous, people will not be degraded but, rather, all will be able to live well. It is also important that employees have a life that is apart from their work and that gives them access to resources and facilities that are not dependent on their employers.

Our third concern can be expressed simply with the question, *how much wealth* should one have? Here we find that the ideas in Aristotle's *Politics* diverge greatly from those found under what we have called the Idea of the Modern State, and the point of divergence is money. If wealth is measured in perishable goods such as food or even livestock, a natural limit on possessions exerts itself. One should have as much as one needs for living, but to take more so that it spoils and is wasted is greed. Similarly with land, a natural limit is the amount of land that one can effectively use. The invention of money, however, changes things, because money can be stored and does not spoil. So, it could seem that there is no reason not to accumulate and store as much as possible. As we saw earlier, there is something strange in this, because money proves useful only when it is spent, and others have noted that it is ridiculous to have boxes of gold stored away but no food. On the other hand, in the modern world, one cannot build factories and produce goods for sale without access to large amounts of saved money. The fact remains that the invention of money changed the possibilities in regard to how much wealth a person might accumulate.

Aristotle's response is that possessions, including money, are for the sake of life, both life itself and living well. He insists that we should live 'with moderation and liberally,'[7] as both virtues are necessary. By *moderation*, he means the virtue also called *temperance* that disposes us to self-restraint in matters of pleasure and pain, a mean between licentiousness and insensibility. The more common failing is to become licentious or to indulge in too much pleasure. By *liberality*, he means the virtue that disposes us to balance our acquisition and spending of money. It leads us neither to spend more than we earn nor to amass wealth needlessly. A liberal life is marked by generosity to others.

---

7.   Aristotle, *Politics* II, 6 (1265a33), 65.

The modern philosopher, John Locke, took a very different view. Since wealth was no longer measured in things that were perishable and because liberty was his major presupposition, he proposed that wealth measured in terms of money and things, including land, which could be converted into money, should have no moral limit. He assumed that natural resources, particularly land, were effectively inexhaustible, so that total wealth would always increase. That is an assumption that is now being challenged by population growth and by global environmental issues.

This chapter has investigated business and wealth. Much more could be said, especially about how to acquire and manage wealth, but that belongs to the study of economics. The point of the chapter has been to recognise that a country needs wealth at every level of its life, and to identify the various forms of wealth. The political challenge is to use wealth so that people, families, villages, towns, cities and countries are enabled to live well. This can in part be provided for by ensuring that the majority of people are moderately well off and that the very wealthy and the very poor are few in numbers.

Chapter Ten
What Is the Good for Pacific Life?

As we come to the end of our survey of Aristotle's political thought, it is right to return by way of final reflection to the theme of the *good*, which has been with us for most of our investigation. In Aristotelian terms, if we are going to engage in action, we need to be clear both about the end or the good that we are pursuing and about the way in which we can achieve it. The core activity of politics is building the political community through negotiation and careful articulation of laws, policies and decisions. In order to be effective, we need a clear understanding of the good both of persons and of communities.

In this chapter, we will first review what Aristotle has said about the good in the *Politics*. Then we will contrast this with the senses of the good articulated by early modern philosophers under the notion of the Idea of the Modern State. Finally, we will raise questions about how the good might be thought about in Pacific countries.

Aristotle on the Good

In Book I, Aristotle points out that the highest and most authoritative community, namely the political community or country, aims at the most authoritative good of all. In the move from life in isolated villages to a co-operative life of many villages gathered into a single community, the goal is self-sufficiency but not simply in terms of material necessities. 'While coming into being for the sake of living, [the political community] exists for the sake of living well.'[1] Fruitful political activity depends on serious thought about what 'well' means.

---

1. Aristotle, *Politics* I, 2 (1252b30), 37, substituting 'political community' for 'city'.

What are the goods that we seek? It is a question that political leaders ought frequently to discuss.

The basis of these claims lies in nature. While human beings are in many ways bound by nature and therefore destined to labour for the necessities of life, such as food and shelter, nature also gives them the ability to reason and to speak. The human voice is not simply an indicator of pleasure and pain, as sounds are for animals, but is rather able to articulate senses of the advantageous and the harmful, the good and the bad, the just and the unjust. This again is the basis of Aristotle's claim that the human being is a political animal. It is only in the political community that the possibilities of this kind of life can be worked out. And so, as we saw in Chapter Two, Aristotle is able to say that 'one who is incapable of participating or who is in need of nothing through being self-sufficient is no part of a country and so is either a beast or a god'.[2]

The shape of the human community is, however, not determined by nature, though its limits are specified by such things as human desire, capability and difference. It is put together through human collaboration, judgement and decision. In Books IV to VI, Aristotle explores some of the choices that could be made to allow human beings to live freely in relation to one another, 'ruling and being ruled', governed politically rather than despotically. In Book VII, he begins, 'Concerning the best [constitution], one who is going to undertake the investigation appropriate to it must necessarily discuss first what the most choice-worthy life is'.[3]

As we saw in Chapter Seven, Aristotle shows in Books IV to VI a deep realism about what different groups in the community will seek. At the most basic level, the democrats seek freedom to do whatever they like; the oligarchs seek wealth; aristocrats seek virtue; the well-born seek honour and nobility; tyrants seek power and pleasure. Each of these has a partial grasp of the good and consequently of what is just and so alone will get into difficulty. The art of the legislator and founder of a political community is to balance each of these parts of a community, so that each can acknowledge a certain justice in the outcome and so that each can contribute in a way that is effective for the life of the community. If the middling element of the population

---

2. Aristotle, *Politics* I, 2 (1253a28), 37.
3. Aristotle, *Politics* VII, 1 (1323b14), 197, substituting 'constitution' for 'regime'.

is increased and strengthened, as in the best practicable constitution of Book IV, that is, the republic, a kind of virtue, in which a mean is found between extremes, will obtain both for persons and for the country as a whole.

It is, perhaps, of this kind of community that Aristotle speaks in a more relaxed way in the *Rhetoric*. There he gives an itemised list of what he calls the 'non-controversially good things'. Again, this is not a definitive list, and it appears a little untidy, but it is useful in expanding our vision of what might be considered under the good. He lists:

> Happiness: it is intrinsically eligible and self-sufficient and we choose many things for its sake
> Justice, courage, restraint, magnanimity, splendour and the other similar dispositions: they are virtues of the soul. Also health and beauty and such like: they are bodily virtues and productive of many advantages . . . Wealth: it is the virtue of possession and brings many advantages.
> Friendship and the friend: the friend is intrinsically eligible and also brings many advantages.
> Status and reputation: these are pleasant and advantageous and are, for the most part, accompanied by those things that earn them. Verbal and practical capacity: all such things bring advantages.
> Also native wit, memory, aptitude to learn, quick wits and so on: these capacities all have good consequences.
> Even being alive: intrinsically eligible, even if no other advantages were to come of it.
> Also justice: a kind of communal expediency.[4]

It is a list that may suit most people, yet we still have to think carefully about the goods that are most important to us and to our communities.

Returning to the more formal analysis of the *Politics*, in Book VII, Aristotle examines the good without 'presupposition but unqualifiedly',[5] that is, not with the limitations of the views of the groups listed in the last paragraph, but in terms of what is really the best human life. As we saw in Chapter Five, he distinguishes three kinds of good: *external goods*—property, wealth, reputation; *goods of*

---

4. Aristotle, *Rhetoric* I, 6 (1362b10–27), 92–3.
5. Aristotle, *Politics* VII, 13 (1332a10), 217.

the body—health, beauty, pleasure; *goods of the soul*—the intellectual and moral virtues. One who is truly blessed will have each of these in adequate proportion. Although he does not develop a list of these goods in any detail, we should take his lead seriously and examine in detail each of the kinds of good that are part of a happy life. The area on which he does expand is the tension between external goods and virtue. He notes that people generally cannot get enough of external goods but are easily satisfied with a modicum of virtue. This is the basis of the presuppositions noted above, and he insists that it is an error of judgement. External things are useful instruments to life but in excess they are either harmful or simply not beneficial and so should be had in moderation. The things of the soul—knowledge and understanding and the moral virtues, particularly moderation, justice, courage and prudence—do not admit of excess and should be sought energetically both by persons and by the political community.

Modern Senses of the Good

The intellectual movement that we have characterised as the Idea of the Modern State, and that has had enormous impact on the Western world, stands in significant contrast to the Aristotelian position. The direction was set by Machiavelli, when he wrote the following in his little book, *The Prince*:

> Many have dreamed up republics and principalities which have never in truth been known to exist; the gulf between how one should live and how one does live is so wide that a man who neglects what is actually done for what should be done moves towards self-destruction rather than self-preservation. The fact is that a man who wants to act virtuously in every way necessarily comes to grief among so many who are not virtuous. Therefore if a prince wants to maintain his rule he must be prepared not to be virtuous, and to make use of this or not according to need.[6]

---

6.   Machiavelli, *The Prince*, chapter 15, page 50.

With this short statement, Machiavelli inverted political ideals. It was not that he acknowledged human failure in virtue, as had Aristotle, but that he proposed that virtue as traditionally understood was not a good in the political world. The prince would seek power and then do whatever he wanted to do with what was at his disposal.

It was Hobbes who followed through on the implications of Machiavelli's move and who most clearly articulated the Idea of the Modern State. His view of human nature implies that people mostly follow their passions and that without a strong government they will simply fall into conflict with one another. It is in seeking peace out of a world of conflict that human beings form a state. The primary motivation and the bond that endures is fear. He expresses the goods sought in the following way:

> The passions that incline men to peace are fear of death; desire of such things as are necessary to commodious living; and hope by their industry to obtain them.[7]

The central good is the achievement of commodious or comfortable living; in Aristotelian terms, goods both external and of the body. Peace is necessary, but maintained under the press of fear and not through any bond of affection. Hobbes assumes that people will be prepared to work industriously if they are thereby able to generate the things that make them comfortable and give them pleasure. He envisages a people who are 'relaxed and comfortable'.[8]

One way in which the difference between the Aristotelian and Hobbesian positions plays out is in discussions between economists and political theorists about development in places such as the Pacific islands. The economist will typically propose that what is most important is to get the economy moving, to make it grow. The political thinker is more likely to say that it is necessary first to balance the constitution so that a settlement is reached and people are generally happy with their share of the common good, whether the country is poor or wealthy. It is a question of competing goods. The chief *political good* is justice; the chief *economic good* is wealth. Both are difficult to achieve. The Hobbesian will emphasise the economic

---

7. Hobbes, *Leviathan*, chapter 13, number 14, page 86.
8. The former Australian Prime Minister, John Howard, frequently used this phrase to express his hopes for the Australian people.

good on the basis that we have just seen. The Aristotelian will insist that both are important, but that they are different kinds of goods. The economic good is a necessary good. Human beings cannot live without adequate food and shelter. It is not, however, what we live *for*. The political good, on the other hand, is an end, a 'that for the sake of which'. We might call it an end in itself, something that gives ultimate direction and meaning to life. People will not be content unless they are able to live together in a way they believe is just. Justice is something for which they will fight.

Locke extended and softened Hobbes' thought and was very influential in the formation of modern countries, especially in the English-speaking world. We have already seen how he proposed that there need be no limit to the amount of wealth that might be accrued by individual people. Locke also proposed that the interests of the state be limited so as not to include such things as religion and, in the absence of harm to others, morality or ethics.

The political culture that has grown out of these developments, namely, *liberal democracy*, has been very successful in allowing people who are different to live together without conflict. It has been particularly successful in providing the conditions for the generation of large economies and of ever-increasing wealth. It remains, however, largely neutral in matters of ethics, except where conflict and harm are concerned. This does not mean that it opposes ethics, but rather that it relegates it to the realm of the private, which is not a matter of public or political interest. Liberal democrats frequently look to religion, also regarded as a private activity, to instruct people in ethical matters. At the present time, however, there seems to be a crisis in the West as the neutrality of the state in relation to ethics is taken as a rejection of any ethics at all, and as a decline in participation in religious belief and practice has set people adrift from another significant source of moral formation.

The Good in Small Island Countries

There is much that separates the small island countries of the Pacific from their larger liberal democratic neighbours, even though they do enter into successful and co-operative relationships with them and must, indeed, deal with the broad challenge of globalisation in its various senses. Some differences are readily discerned. In the Pacific, extended families carry a significance long lost in the West, which generally functions on the basis of the assumed autonomy of isolated individuals. Communities are built on affection rather than on anything like Hobbesian fear. Attitudes to wealth are also clearly different, in terms of both how much wealth one might wish to accumulate and how it might be distributed. Land laws, customs and practices see the land as something intimately connected to families rather than as a commodity that can be easily and quickly sold or exchanged.

Critics readily put these differences down to lack of capacity, with a clear implication that small island countries generally fail to generate the kind of economy necessary for modern life. While there is truth in the observation that small island states are not able to generate gigantic vibrant economies, the claim denies and masks a more significant truth, namely, that Pacific peoples have been able to live successfully on small isolated islands for many hundreds of years. Western tourists visit not simply to swim in the warm ocean waters but to hear the laughter coming from villages and to experience the relaxed hospitality and delicate ritual of the people.

This suggests that Pacific peoples have every right to think about the way in which they want to live and the advantages that they want their countries to provide on their own terms rather than simply being expected to mimic the West. They have to live in a world system of states, but they do not have to do it in the same way as Western countries do. It may be that more co-operative arrangements between small Pacific countries will help them manage some of the global and economic pressures that face them. This may even help them negotiate better terms with their large neighbours. But it is also important that they continue to develop patterns of life that are sustainable on their islands and that are in tune with their traditions and aspirations.

One of the difficulties of following Aristotle's lead on the question of the good is that he gives very little detail. There is always much more that we need to know and to decide. There are two reasons for Aristotle's lack of detail. First, his concern as a philosopher is to begin to think in the right way. What he gives us are categories with which we can think about these things. It is for this reason that the *Politics* begins several times. He wants to teach people how to think about the issues rather than to tell them in detail what they should decide. Secondly, the matters under consideration are practical, so that while the general lines of thought about living in a political community can be clearly articulated, much of the detail can only be filled in at a particular time in a particular place by people who can judge wisely about what is the best thing to do.

My suggestion is that we should think freshly about the three general kinds of goods noted by Aristotle at the beginning of this chapter, but that we should do it in reverse order—the goods of the soul; the goods of the body; external goods. We should do this in the context of the limitations of geography, history and culture that we have explored in this book, and in the context of the questions at the end of Chapter Six, which help us analyse a particular country and constitution.

What are the *goods of the soul* that we would seek in this place at this time? In other words, what constitutes a happy life in this place? What are the intellectual needs of the people? What do they need to learn in order to live successfully? What intellectual and cultural pursuits will themselves give meaning to life? What moral virtues do people need? The answer to these questions will be both general and specific. Clearly, courage will make the list, but what is courage in each particular situation? Courage at war or in a dangerous place is different from the courage one needs to face the day on a peaceful island. What, indeed, are the virtues needed to live successfully in a small village? How are these different from the virtues needed to live in a town or city?

What are the *goods of the body* that we most seek? Clearly, health, strength and beauty will be prized. How are they to be achieved? Where is moderation called for in such matters?

What *external goods* will be important for us? What role has honour to play in building our communities? How much wealth do we need, and how can we live realistically within our means? What kinds of manufactured goods do we want, and how will we afford them? How do we think about land, and are there any changes in thinking that we might anticipate? Do we manage land well and justly?

I have heard it asserted in three Pacific countries that in those countries nobody is poor. What was meant was that in those countries nobody was without family and a place to live and that with land everybody could grow food and live successfully. The contrast was made with large Western countries in which some people sleep on the city streets without shelter and often go without sufficient food and certainly without adequate communal support. There is much that could be said to expand on this assertion, but for our purposes it is an indicator that, despite the material attractions of the modern world, there is much that is not right in it. We need to recognise the richness of life in Pacific countries, where communal bonds of affection are strong and where much about life is good.

Epilogue
In Search of Pacific Traditions of Political Theory and Practice

This book began with the claim that Aristotelian political analysis would help Pacific peoples analyse their political situations so as to enable better political decisions in ways better than much modern political theory could do. That claim has been argued, and the details of the Aristotelian analysis have been spelt out. Yet, another question arises. What of the traditions of political theory and practice of Pacific peoples themselves? Surely these should be taken into account. The Aristotelian analysis makes room for them by giving significant place to culture, to history and to geography in the determination of how a political community might be best organised. More could be done, however, to bring out the lines of Pacific thought and practice.

How might this be done? It will not be an easy task. There is no way of returning to just how things were before both because much has happened and people have changed and because it would be surprising if people today wanted to do that. On the other hand, it would make good sense to search the traditions of song, story and relationship for meanings and understandings that will assist Pacific peoples to enable their political communities to flourish. What sustained thousands of years of successful living on these islands? What is learnt could be incorporated bit by bit into the arrangements and understandings by which people live today. This is a task for Pacific Islanders themselves.

Appendix One
Distribution of Aristotle's Texts
according to the Chapters of This Book

Chapter Number	Chapter Heading and Subheadings	Books and Sections of Aristotle's *Politics*, or of other texts, as noted
One	**Introduction**	*Ethics* I, 1–3; X, 9
Two	**Kinds of Life and the Origins of Political Community**	
	Pre-Political Communities	I, 2
	Political Community	I, 2
	Different Kinds of Rule	I, 1, 3–7, 12–13
Three	**Learning From Experience**	
	Aristotle's Criticism of other Writers	II, 1–8
	The Modern State	
	Analysis of Existing Countries	II, 9–12
Four	**The Life of the Citizen and the Kinds of Constitution**	
	Citizens and Country	III, 1–8
	Possible Constitutions	IV, 1–10
	Political Institutions and Offices	IV, 14–16; VI, 8
Five	**The Best Possible and Best Practicable Constitutions**	
	The Best Possible Constitution	VII, 1–3, 8–10, 13
	The Best Practicable Constitution	IV, 7, 8, 11
	Political Justice	III, 9–13; *Ethics* V

Chapter Number	Chapter Heading and Subheadings	Books and Sections of Aristotle's *Politics*, or of other texts, as noted
Six	**The Material Conditions of Political Life**	
	Material Conditions of a Country	VII, 4–7, 10–12
	Other Senses of the Best Constitution	IV, 12–13
	Monarchy	III, 14–18; V, 10–11
Seven	**Preserving Constitutions and Countries**	
	Variety in Country and Constitution	V, 1; VI, 1–7
	Change and Preservation	V, 1–9, 12; VI, 4 (8)
	The Political Art—Speech-Making	*Rhetoric*
Eight	**Nurturing Political Life—Education**	
	Moral Upbringing—Habituation	*Ethics* I, II, VII
	Basic Education—Instruction	VII, 13–17
	Education for Living Well—The Arts and Culture	VIII, *Ethics* X, *Poetics*
Nine	**Sustaining Political Life—Business and Wealth**	
	Possessions, Land and Money	I, 4, 8–9; II, 5–8; VII, 10
	Household Management, Business and Taxation	I, 8–11; *Economics*
	Ethical Concerns	As for sections 1 and 2 plus *Ethics* V, 2
Ten	**What Is the Good for Pacific Life?**	
	Aristotle on the Good	I, 2; VII, 1 and 13; *Ethics* I, 1–2; *Rhetoric* I, 6.
	Modern Senses of the Good	
	The Good in Small Island Countries	

Appendix Two
Outline of Aristotle's *Politics*

An outline of Aristotle's *Politics* is offered here for those who may like to go on and read the *Politics* itself or who may like to follow up particular ideas and discussions. The history of the manuscripts of the *Politics* is complex and has led some commentators to suggest that the text has been rearranged and corrupted. Some have even tried to reorganise it. My view is that although there are parts of the text missing, such as the later chapters of Book VIII, the *Politics* can be conceived as basically what Aristotle left us, that is, a collection of 'materials of the school' or teaching materials. Apart from some actual losses, the apparent incompleteness of the discussion can be explained by the principles we noted in Chapter One. It is the task of the political philosopher to get the beginnings right. The philosopher will not fill out the detail but will rather leave that to the politician. This outline is constructed with these points in mind.

1. Introduction (*Ethics* X, 9)
2. The Natural Origins of the City (Book I)
   a. Pre-political and political communities (I, 1–2)
   b. The household (I, 3)
   c. Mastery and slavery (I, 4–7)
   d. Wealth and business (I, 8–11)
   e. Household rule (I, 12–13)

3. The Origins of the City in Thought and in Deed (Book II)
   a. The Best Constitution according to Those Who Have Written
      i. Plato's *Republic*—excessive unity versus the city as a multitude (II, 1–5)
      ii. Plato's *Laws*—errors of detail (II, 6)
      iii. Phaleas of Chalcedon—artificial equalisation of property (II, 7)
      iv. Hippodamus of Miletus—artificial divisions (II, 8)
   b. Actual Constitutions that Function Well (II, 9–11)
      i. The Constitution of Sparta—warlike virtue versus luxury (II, 9)
      ii. The Constitution of Crete—advantages of an island (II, 10)
      iii. The Constitution of Carthage—finer detail is critical (II, 11)
   c. Examples of Other Constitutions and Legislators (II, 12)
4. Formal Examination of the Political Possibilities of a City (Book III)
   a. City and Citizenship (III, 1–5)
      i. Definitions of city and citizen (III, 1–2)
      ii. Questions about the identity of the city (III, 3)
      iii. Virtue of the good citizen and the good person (III, 4)
      iv. Settling questions about citizenship (III, 5)
   b. Formal Division of Kinds of Constitution and Their Basis (III, 6–8)
      i. Political rule distinguished from mastery (III, 6)
      ii. Three correct (monarchy, aristocracy and republicanism) and three deviant constitutions (tyranny, oligarchy and democracy) (III, 7)
      iii. Deviant constitutions distinguished on the basis of poverty and wealth (III, 8)
   c. The Nature of Political Justice and Its Problems (III, 9–13)
      i. Partiality of oligarchic and democratic justice (III, 9)
      ii. Problems with law and justice and with distribution of political voice (III, 10–11)
      iii. Achieving just distribution in the context of equality and difference (III, 12–13)
   d. Monarchy and the Rule of Law (III, 14–17)

     i. Different kinds of monarchy (III, 14)

     ii. Justice of the rule of one—rule by a person or rule by law (III, 15)

     iii. Arguments against monarchy (III, 16)

     iv. Possibility of just kingship (III, 17)

  e. Conclusion (incomplete) (III, 18)

5. Political Science: Detailed Examination of the Political Possibilities of the City (Books IV–VI)

  a. Closer Study of Constitutions and Their Institutions (Book IV)

     i. Scope of political science and the four senses of the best constitution (IV, 1–2)

     ii. Parts of the city and basis for distinguishing kinds of constitution (IV, 3)

     iii. More detailed analysis of the kinds of constitution (IV, 4–10)

        1. Kinds of democracy and oligarchy (IV, 4–6)

        2. Kinds of aristocracy and republic (IV, 7–9)

        3. Kinds of tyranny (IV, 10)

     iv. The best practicable constitution—the republic with a large middle (IV, 11)

     v. Other senses of the best—what particular peoples can achieve (IV, 12–13)

     vi. Institutions and offices available for distribution (IV, 14–16)

        1. Deliberative institutions and offices (IV, 14)

        2. Executive institutions and offices (IV, 15)

        3. Judicial institutions and offices (IV, 16)

  b. Preservation and Destruction of Constitutions and Cities (Book V)

     i. Destruction of Constitutions (IV, 1–7)

        1. Sources of instability, faction and revolution (V, 1–4)

        2. Destruction of democracies (V, 5)

        3. Destruction of oligarchies (V, 6)

        4. Destruction of aristocracies (V, 7)

     ii. Preserving constitutions (IV, 8–11)

        1. Preservation of constitutions in general (IV, 89)

i. Necessity and public nature of education (VIII, 1)
ii. The content and manner of education (VIII, 2)
iii. Education for noble leisure (VIII, 3)
iv. Gymnastic education (VIII, 4)
v. Musical education (VIII, 5-6)
vi. The effect of music on character (VIII, 7)

Note that Book VIII is incomplete.

Appendix Three
Comparative Data for
Pacific Island Countries and Territories

Country or Territory	Land Area (sq km)	Population (2013 est)	GNP per Person ($US)	Constitutional Arrangements * Member state of United Nations in its own right ^ Member state of Pacific Forum in its own right
MELANESIA				
Fiji Islands	18,274	896,758	4,900	*^ Republic
New Caledonia	18,275	264,022	37,700	Territorial collective of France
Papua New Guinea	462,840	6,431,902	2,800	*^ Parliamentary democracy in the Commonwealth
Solomon Islands	28,896	597,248	3,400	*^ Parliamentary democracy in the Commonwealth
Vanuatu	12,189	261,565	5,000	*^ Parliamentary republic
POLYNESIA				
American Samoa	199	54,719	8,000	Unincorporated organised territory of the USA
Cook Islands	236	10,447	9,100	^ Self-governing in free association with New Zealand
French Polynesia	4,167	277,293	22,000	Parliamentary representative democratic French collectivity
Hawaii	16,635	1,374,810	48,727	State of the USA
Niue	260	1,229	5,800	^ Self-governing in free association with New Zealand

Country or Territory	Land Area (sq km)	Population (2013 est)	GNP per Person ($US)	Constitutional Arrangements * Member state of United Nations in its own right ^ Member state of Pacific Forum in its own right
Norfolk Island	36	2,196	NA	Self-governing territory of Australia
Pitcairn Islands	47	48	NA	Overseas territory of UK
Samoa	2,831	195,476	6,300	*^ Parliamentary democracy
Tokelau	12	1,353	1,000	Self-administering territory of New Zealand
Tonga	747	106,322	7,700	*^ Constitutional monarchy
Tuvalu	26	10,698	3,400	*^ Parliamentary democracy in the Commonwealth
Wallis and Futuna	142	15,507	3,800	Overseas territory of France
MICRONESIA				
Commonwealth of Northern Mariana Islands	464	51,170	13,600	Commonwealth in political union with the USA
Federated States of Micronesia	702	106,104	7,500	*^ Constitutional government in free association with the USA
Guam	544	160,378	28,700	Organised unincorporated territory of the USA
Kiribati	811	103,248	6,100	*^ Republic
Nauru	21	9,434	5,000	*^ Republic
Palau	459	21,108	10,500	*^ Constitutional government in free association with the USA
Republic of Marshall Islands	181	69,747	8,800	*^ Constitutional government in free association with the USA

Sources: CIA, *World Fact Book*, at <https://www.cia.gov/library/publications/the-world-factbook/geos/ps.html>, accessed 29 July 2013. Hawaii data from 2011 State of Hawai'i Data Book at < http://dbedt.hawaii.gov/economic/databook/db2011/>, accessed 29 July 2013.

All countries or territories listed except Hawaii and Norfolk Island are members of the Pacific Community. Australia, France, New Zealand and the United States of America are members of the Pacific Community. Australia and New Zealand are members of the Pacific Forum.

Appendix Four
Maps of Pacific Countries and Territories

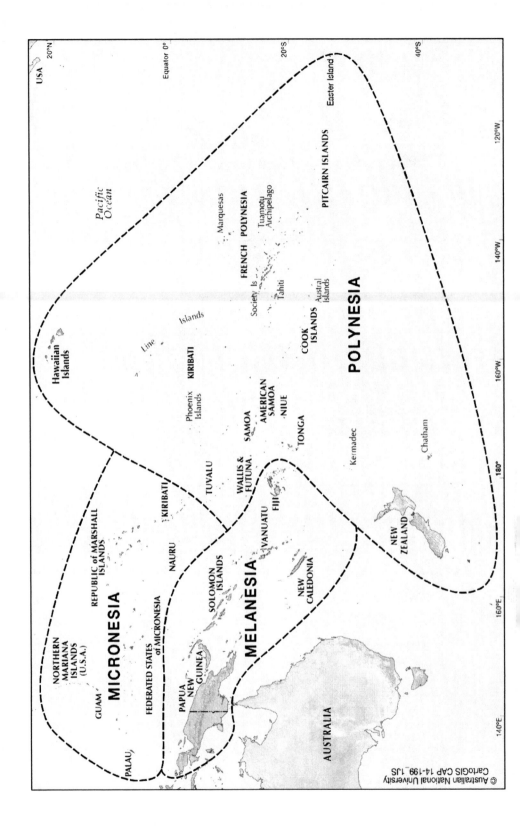

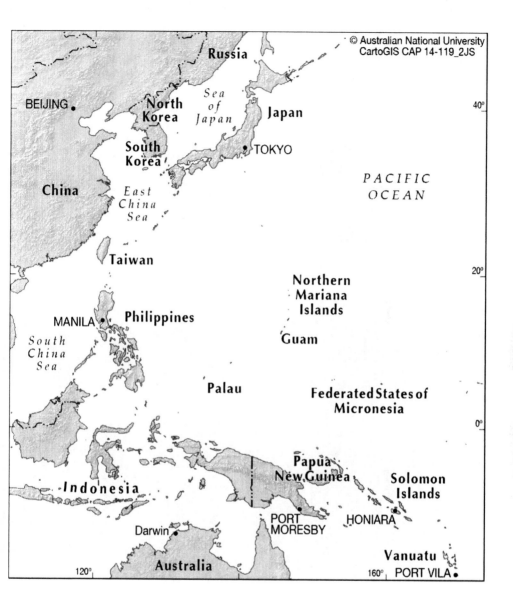

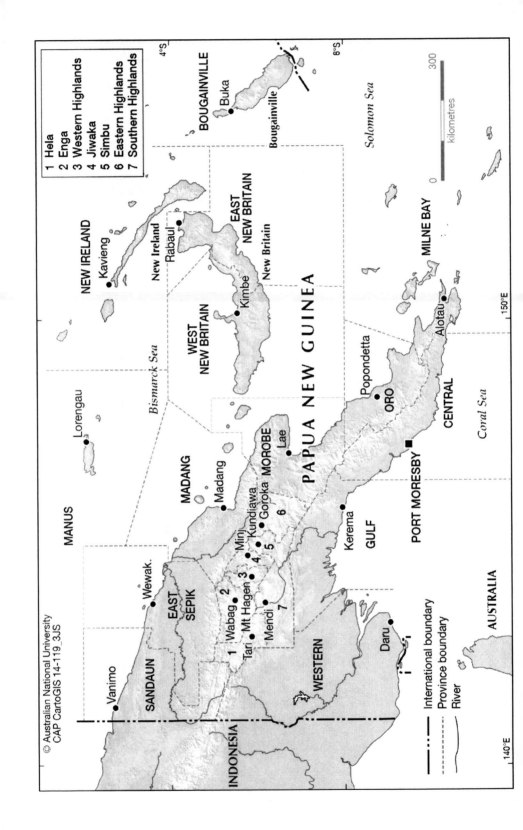

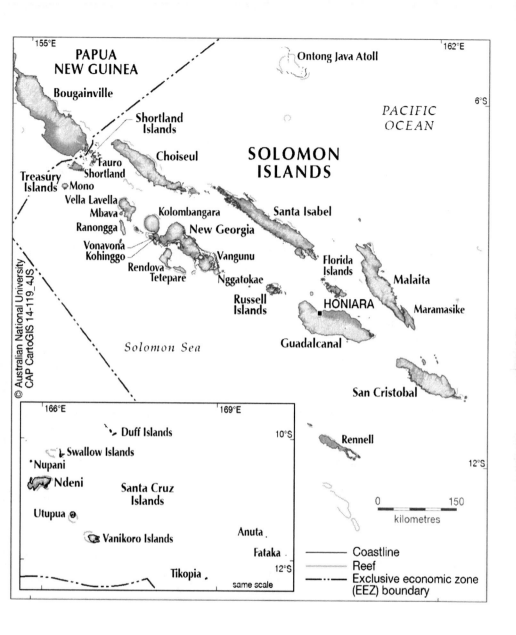

PAPUA
NEW GUINEA

Bougainville

Ontong Java Atoll

PACIFIC
OCEAN

6°S

Shortland
Islands

Choiseul

SOLOMON
ISLANDS

Fauro
Treasury Shortland
Islands Mono

Vella Lavella
Mbava
Ranongga

Kolombangara

Santa Isabel

New Georgia

Vonavona
Kohinggo
Rendova
Tetepare

Vangunu

Florida
Islands

Malaita

Nggatokae

HONIARA

Maramasike

Russell
Islands

Solomon Sea

Guadalcanal

San Cristobal

166°E

169°E

Duff Islands

10°S

Rennell

Swallow Islands

Nupani

12°S

Ndeni

Santa Cruz
Islands

0   150
kilometres

Utupua

Vanikoro Islands

Anuta

Fataka

Tikopia

12°S

same scale

————— Coastline
————— Reef
—··—·· Exclusive economic zone
        (EEZ) boundary

155°E

162°E

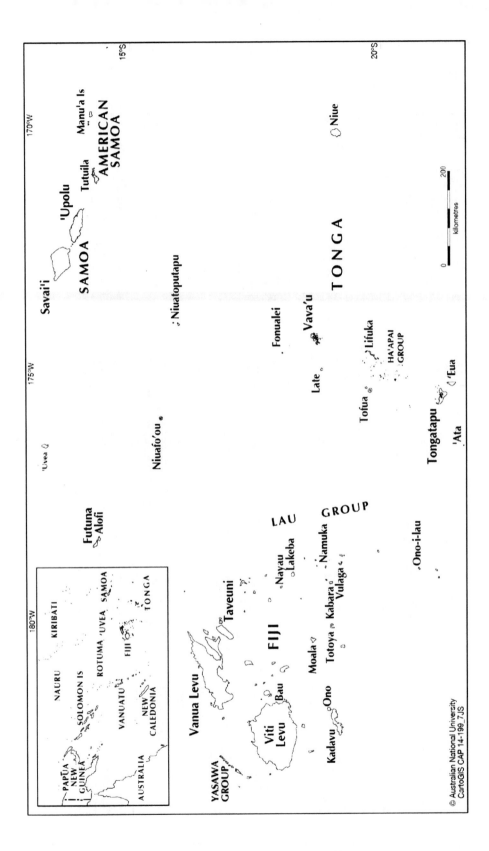

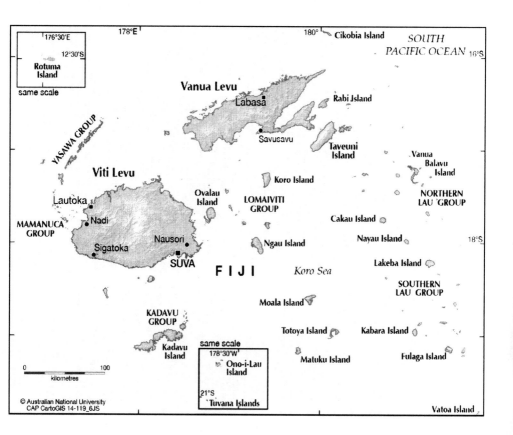

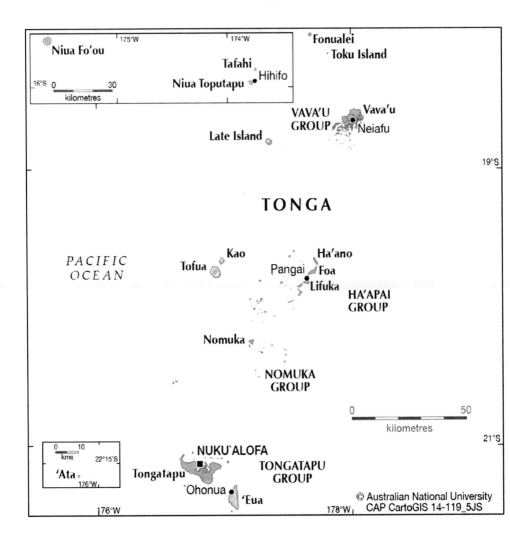

Niua Fo'ou

175°W   174°W

Tafahi
Niua Toputapu   Hihifo

16°S   0   30
         kilometres

Fonualei
Toku Island

VAVA'U   Vava'u
GROUP   Neiafu

Late Island

19°S

TONGA

PACIFIC
OCEAN

Kao   Ha'ano
Tofua   Pangai   Foa
                     Lifuka
                     HA'APAI
                     GROUP

Nomuka

NOMUKA
GROUP

0   50
         kilometres

21°S

0   10
  kms   22°15'S
'Ata
  176°W

NUKU`ALOFA

Tongatapu   TONGATAPU
`Ohonua   GROUP
        'Eua

© Australian National University
CAP CartoGIS 14-119_5JS

176°W   178°W

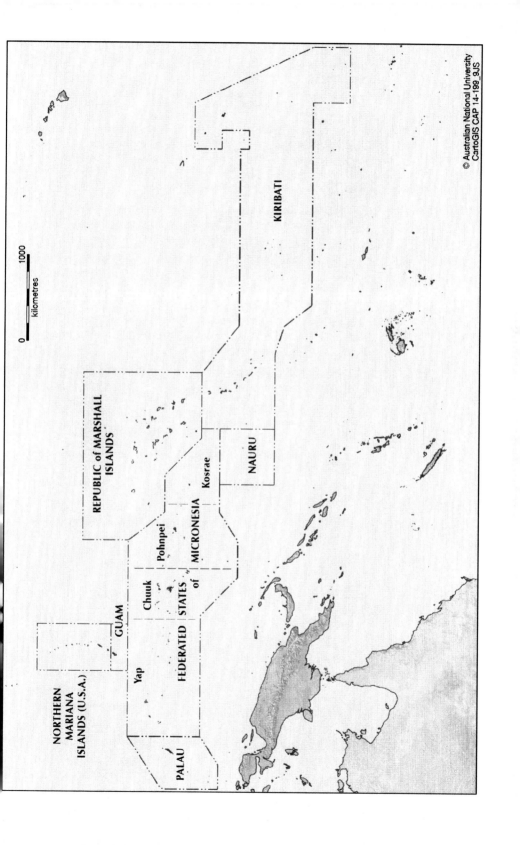

NORTHERN MARIANA ISLANDS (U.S.A.)

GUAM

Yap

PALAU

Chuuk

FEDERATED STATES of MICRONESIA

Pohnpei

Kosrae

REPUBLIC of MARSHALL ISLANDS

NAURU

KIRIBATI

0   1000
kilometres

© Australian National University
CartoGIS CAP 14-199_9JS

. Farallon de Pajaros

International boundary

0   kilometres   100

. Maug Islands

20°N

. Asuncion

NORTHERN MARIANA
ISLANDS (U.S.A.)

Agrihan

*Pacific
Ocean*

Pagan

Alamagan

Guguan

17°N

Sarigan

Philippine Sea

Anatahan

, Farallon de Medinilla

CAPITOL HILL
Saipan

Tinian

Aguijan

Rota

14°N

HAGATNA
GUAM (U.S.A.)

Cocos Island

© Australian National University
Base map CAP 12-256_8JS

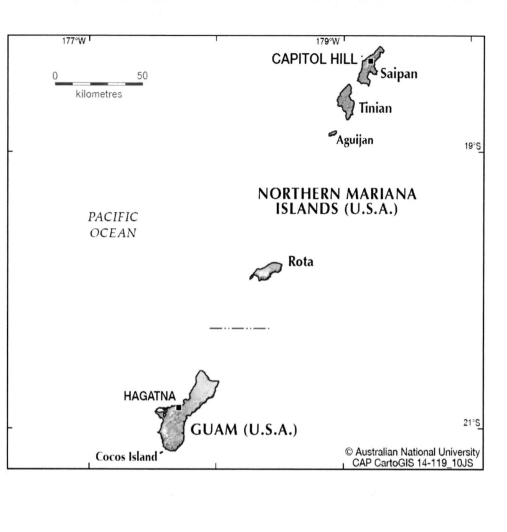

Selected Bibliography

Translations of Aristotle's Works

Aristotle. *The Art of Rhetoric*. Translated by HC Hawson-Tancred. London: Penguin, 2004.

Aristotle. *The Complete Works of Aristotle: The Revised Oxford Translation*. Edited by Jonathan Barnes. 2 volumes. Princeton, NJ: Princeton University Press, 1985.

Aristotle. *Economics*. In *The Complete Works of Aristotle: The Revised Oxford Translation*. Edited by Jonathan Barnes. Volume II, 2130–51. Princeton, NJ: Princeton University Press, 1985.

Aristotle. *The Nicomachean Ethics*. Translated by JAK Thomson and revised by Hugh Tredennick. London: Penguin, 2004.

Aristotle. *Poetics*. In *The Complete Works of Aristotle: The Revised Oxford Translation*. Edited by Jonathan Barnes. Volume II, 2316–40. Princeton, NJ: Princeton University Press, 1985.

Aristotle. *The Politics*. Translated with an introduction by Carnes Lord. Chicago: University of Chicago Press, 1984.

Aristotle. *The Politics*. Translated by TA Sinclair and revised by Trevor J Saunders. London: Penguin, 1992.

Aristotle. *The Politics of Aristotle*. Translated with introduction, notes and analysis by Peter L Phillips Simpson. Chapel Hill: University of North Carolina Press, 1997.

Commentaries on Aristotle's Works

Bates, Clifford Angell, Jr. *Aristotle's 'Best Regime': Kingship, Democracy, and the Rule of Law*. Baton Rouge: Louisiana State University Press, 2003.

Davis, Michael. *The Politics of Philosophy: A Commentary on Aristotle's Politics*. Lanham, MD: Rowman and Littlefield, 1996.

Garver, Eugene. *Aristotle's Politics: Living Well and Living Together*. Chicago: University of Chicago Press, 2011.

Johnson, Curtis N. *Aristotle's Theory of State*. New York: St Martin's Press, 1990.

Keyt, David, and Fred D Miller. *A Companion to Aristotle's Politics*. Cambridge, MA: Blackwell, 1991.

Lord, Carnes. *Education and Culture in the Political Thought of Aristotle*. Ithaca, NY: Cornell University Press, 1982.

Mulgan, RG. *Aristotle's Political Theory: An Introduction for Students of Political Theory*. Oxford: Clarendon Press, 1977.

Nichols, Mary P. *Citizens and Statesmen: A Study of Aristotle's Politics*. Savage, MD: Rowman and Littlefield, 1992.

Simpson, Peter L Phillips. *A Philosophical Commentary on the Politics of Aristotle*. Chapel Hill: University of North Carolina Press, 1998.

Other Works on Aristotle

Kraut, Richard, and Steven Skultety, editors. *Aristotle's Politics: Critical Essays*. Lanham, MD: Rowman and Littlefield, 2005.

Rorty, Amélie Oksenberg, editor. *Essays on Aristotle's Ethics*. Berkeley: University of California Press, 1980.

———, editor. *Essays on Aristotle's Rhetoric*. Berkeley: University of California Press, 1996.

Shields, Christopher. *Aristotle*. London: Routledge, 2007.

Tressitore, Aristide, editor. *Aristotle and Modern Politics: The Persistence of Political Philosophy*. Notre Dame, IN: University of Notre Dame Press, 2002.

Pacific Studies

Campbell, Ian C. *Worlds Apart: A History of the Pacific Islands.* Christchurch: Canterbury University Press, 2003.

Crocombe, Ron. *The South Pacific.* Suva: Institute of Pacific Studies, University of the South Pacific, 2001.

Fischer, Steven Roger. *A History of the Pacific Islands.* Houndsmills: Palgrave, 2002.

Jowitt, Anita, and Tess Newton Cain. *Passage of Change: Law, Society and Governance in the Pacific.* Canberra: Pandanus Books, 2003.

Lal, Brig V, and Kate Fortune. *The Pacific Islands: An Encyclopedia.* Honolulu: University of Hawai'i Press, 2000.

Narokobi, Bernard. *Law and Custom in Melanesia.* Suva: University of the South Pacific and Goroka: Melanesian Institute, 1989.

Nunn, Patrick D. *Pacific Island Landscapes.* Suva: Institute of Pacific Studies, University of the South Pacific, 1998.

Paterson, Don. *Selected Constitutions of the South Pacific.* Suva: Institute of Justice and Applied Legal Studies, 2000.

Rewi, Poia. *Whaikōrero: The World of Māori Oratory.* Auckland: Auckland University Press, 2010.

State, Society and Governance in Melanesia. Discussion Papers 1996–2010. <http://ips.cap.anu.edu/ssgm/publications/>. Accessed 2 September 2015.

Index

For references to parts of Aristotle's *Politics, Ethics, Rhetoric* or *Poetics*, see pp 157–8. For *geographic, demographic, economic* and *constitutional data* for Pacific countries and territories, see pp 165–7. For *maps* of Pacific countries and territories, see pp 169–79.

R

rationalism 38, 99–100
realism and constitutional blends 68
regime 9
representation, proportional 61
representative democracy 50
representative government 45
republic 66–7
   democracy and 67
   politeia 9
Republic, the (Plato)
   perfect country in 35–7
republicanism 48
respect 81, 143
revolutionary position/viewpoint
   99–100
rhetoric 100–3
   definition of 101
   kinds of 101–2
rights, human 30
Rogers, Robert F
   Destiny's Landfall 124
Rota 118, 119
rule
   kinds of 16–18
   of law 49, 80
   by those in office 49, 80

S

Saipan 118, 119, 125, 126, 129
   Battle of 126
Sālote, Queen (of Tonga) *see* Tupou
   III, Queen Sālote (of Tonga)
Samoa/Samoans 44, 77, 84, 121
San Vitores, Fr Diego Luis de 120
science 112
Second Treatise on Government
   (Locke) 39
security 75
self-sufficiency 74, 145
servants 15
   and masters 138, 142

services, access to 96–7
slavery 12–13n2, 15
social contract 70n5
Socrates 35
Solomon Islands/Islanders 26, 27n8,
   29, 31, 44
   as one country 36
soul, goods of the 148, 152
South Seas Development Company
   (NKK) 125
sovereign (an individual or assembly)
   39–40
sovereignty 40–1
Spain/Spanish 119–20
Spanish–American War 120
Sparta 41–2
speech-making 100–3
spiritedness 76, 113
state-building 29–30
states
   failed or weak 1
   meanings of 'state' 40–1
subjects and citizens 16–18
subsistence economies 96

T

Tāufa'ahau, King (of Tonga) *see*
   Tupou IV, King Tāufa'ahau (of
   Tonga); Tupou V, King Tāufa'ahau
   (of Tonga)
taxation 140
temperance 143
territories
   boundaries of 75
   incorporated or unincorporated
   (USA) 122–3, 124
   size of 74–5
   see also land
theory of the Modern State *see* Idea of
   the Modern State
thoughtfulness 76
Tinian 118
Tonga 44, 77, 79, 83

CPSIA information can be obtained
at www.ICGtesting.com
Printed in the USA
FFOW04n1951260416
23567FF